Daily Conversations with My Interloper

Healthy Exercises in Ennui and Malaise

G. A. Powell Jr.

Hamilton Books
A member of
THE ROWMAN & LITTLEFIELD PUBLISHING GROUP
Lanham • Boulder • New York • Toronto • Plymouth, UK

Copyright © 2008 by
Hamilton Books
4501 Forbes Boulevard
Suite 200
Lanham, Maryland 20706
Hamilton Books Acquisitions Department (301) 459-3366

Estover Road
Plymouth PL6 7PY
United Kingdom

All rights reserved
Printed in the United States of America
British Library Cataloging in Publication Information Available

Library of Congress Control Number: 2007937457
ISBN-13: 978-0-7618-3887-6 (paperback : alk. paper)
ISBN-10: 0-7618-3887-2 (paperback : alk. paper)

∞™ The paper used in this publication meets the minimum
requirements of American National Standard for Information
Sciences—Permanence of Paper for Printed Library Materials,
ANSI Z39.48—1984

Dedicated to

My wife, A. Powell; son, G. E. Powell; friend, A. Kopperude; Dr. A. Alcott.

A Healthy Sequence of Thoughts

1	The 'A' Book—Impious Thoughts	1
	Impious Confessions	1
	Empty Transitions	9
	Platonic Advice on Love and Virtue	10
	Errant Confessions Out of Convulsion	11
	Examinations in the Dark 1–11: Childhood Visions	15
	Anathemas and Self-Deception	18
	–E.M. Cioran: Some Thoughts	20
2	The 'B' book—Sanguine Thoughts for a Hapless World	31
	Some Thoughts on Futility, Ennui, Quotidian, and Consciousness	31
3	The 'C' Book—Thoughts on Bergman, Unamuno, and Camus	44
	Thoughts on Ingmar Bergman(1957): The Seventh Seal	44
	Thoughts on Miguel de Unamuno (1954)	45
	Errant thoughts on Albert Camus	45
4	The 'D' Book—Ennui, Quotidian, and Utopianism	46
	Quotidian, Ennui, and the American: A Postscript	46
	A Tribute to Emile Cioran: Unpublished Essay 2006–2007	46
	Procession of Sub-Men	63
	Quosuque Eadem?	63
	Lucid Dreams	64

The unimportance of anything,	65
Piety	65
Idle	66
(...Ennui...)	66
......x....=.....?	67
5 The 'E' Book—Broken letters and correspondence to and from 'X'	69
References	83

Chapter One

The 'A' Book—Impious Thoughts

I find it irreverent to pray for salvation
—G. A. Powell 2003

IMPIOUS CONFESSIONS

All literary pieces are confessions derived from guilt, shame, and inferiority. This piece is no different.

*

How does one think beyond the language he or she uses?

*

Is creativity the abandonment of language?

*

Most ideas that are worth grappling with are beyond language, not expression —thus the artist.

*

If the ineffable exist, perhaps it is only the artist who knows.

*

Every compulsion is muddled in the ineffable—a struggle for authenticity.

*

Accuracy has never been my intention, only discovery through chaos.

*

Wittgenstein said it best—"the world is all that is the case". Philosophical circles thought his treatise was brilliant. Years later, he reneged. We agreed. He then proceeded to write another treatise. We thought this was brilliant. Recanting philosophical problems, he opted for an agrarian life.

*

All of the world's best thinkers and expatiators have never solved the world's most pressing issues; they simply enumerated them.

*

Human progress is a myth. What has progressed is the amplification of *power, war,* and *greed*.

*

Prove me wrong—tell me 'no,' and what have you proved? The highways are still congested, the sky is still blue—I will have a glass of red wine, please.

*

Vodka, coffee, and Belgium beer, my panacea for living

*

Theories—those who experienced collegial education are familiar with them. We recited them like catechisms. Stained in our mind, are they not spurious? Where are the original thinkers? Are they not to be found in institutions of higher learning?

*

Examine the beggar.

*

Apology: I would like to apologize to the world for baring my presence, influence, and most of all, me.

*

What is a writer but a literary prostitute?

*

Every novel, film, and poem is a reminder of how vile I really am. I love *the Artists,* for their critique lacks effulgence—it's brutal and forthright.

*

Yes, it is difficult to write anything certain or think about certainty. Do we really believe what we believe or know what we know? We just speak about ideas and perceptions with indecipherable metaphoric prose and convoluted ironies.

*

My life—a Francois Truffaut film.

*

Would you like me if I was perfect?

*

Sometimes I wonder what it would be like to be in a center. A center not by perspective but a center where everything is held together: gravity, sin, death, and birth—a center where there are no centers of a center, but *a* center. What lies beyond a metaphysical, existential, and theological center?

*

Modern day bookstores are cemeteries—both the dead and alive are buried. We eulogize them by consuming their texts.

*

Bottom nature—underlying subjectivity not even aware of itself; writing and thinking are wishful attempts to unlock a bottom nature. What would one find, discover, or wish to forget beyond all memory?

*

The daily ritual of seeing something four hundred times is knowing that the four hundred first time will repeat the first.

*

Bewildering to think that I am so close to ending my humanity.

*

The possession of a thing is only as fulfilling as the desire or attention bestowed upon its loss.

*

Today, I stole the last flame from the gods and embarked upon resignation. Alas, my soul belongs to no one!

*

I commit myself to the highest order of nonbeing—to live without the comfort that language affords.

*

All thinkers are preoccupied with one question that justifies their existence. Sartre—freedom, Heideggar—*Dasein,* Camus—suicide, Kierkeggard—faith, and Cioran—history.

*

Imperfections and limitations, knowing this, he remains silent. Agitated, he thinks. His thoughts swell and we see the culmination of wrinkles on his forehead, like the waves before they disappear. My conclusion is that our lecturer, the intellectual, is without hope—he knows his adversary, he 'X' sees his persecutor, the very sword he makes love to will persecute him . . . for the very thing he loves and desires will kill him. His turmoil is not imaginary.

*

My world is one that ignores details.

*

The scholar is condemned. The intellectual is condemned to be free.

*

The question always repeats itself—who are you?

*

God bless hermeneutics, coincidence or fate.

*

The thought of suicide brings us one step closer to the devil, while the act of suicide brings us one step closer to God.

*

Thinkers are different from writers—writers are prostitutes. Thinkers want to be prostitutes.

*

Lyricism is the case when philosophy, mysticism, and rhetoric have failed.

*

Postmodern thought taught us that chaos is possible. Lyricism teaches us that chaos is eminent.

*

I want to tie your lips into a knot so that you will never speak.

*

Existenz is based on the transient moments in which communication is perfect. I have never existed.

*

Now speak!! Yes, you struggle with words. Now we are equals.

*

The institution has made me hate myself; my pen reminds me of this.

*

When asleep, I had glossed over a set of interesting ideas and concepts for you. I am awake now. How unfortunate.

*

Renouncing this world at the age of 18 has caused much strife; all I think about is quietism, retirement, and suicide.

*

What is one to do when the seductive veil no longer exists—when meaning, acquisition, and verve are no longer the case?

*

What I learned at 18 has not changed at the age of 29.

*

History and philosophy are but mere records of human temperament, folly, manipulation, and debauchery.

*

God cursed me with memory.

*

I detest authors who occupy my life for months without end, without apology, leaving no point of exit. Those are months I could use to learn French. I prefer aphorisms and poems, which say what it is they have to say. Even if the tongue is strange, it is okay. . . . I love confusion. I apologize if I am doing the same. At this point, I invite the reader to depart permanently from the text. I understand if you would rather occupy your moments with other pressing issues. It is not my point to press my concerns or inadequacies on you. Why can't authors apologize for their misconduct? I would like an apology from the authors who have acted inappropriately.

*

6   *Chapter One*

I would like to invite Mephistopheles Camus, Cioran, Bergman, and Kierkegaard over for café or red.

*

There are issues that need addressing. The problem with books is that their authors are always on sabbatical. That s/he is never physically present occupies my space when I have pressing question is irritating. Why do we even need to know who the author is. Any author's work is the mere penmanship, craftsmanship of any given set of inspirations. The vestige of Cioran or Nietzsche is the working of those who have agitated them. So, both Cioran and Nietzsche owe much ado to Aristotle and God as they do
to the homeless person who winced at them .

*

My ideas are nothing but fraudulent and imperfect wishes, my graduate teachers have told me.

*

Morning lends us the chance to make a ritual out of life once more over again. A perpetual mode of repetition—the same thoughts guised in unseen metaphors.

*

How foolish. The limitations or the exhausting of a paradigm: man's attempt to omit his inadequacies, his inability to see, feel, smell, and think.

*

Yes, vestiges of Emerson run through me.

*

Books have a way of deterring one's authenticity; read them rashly, rather than vigilantly.

*

I know the enthymeme, the syllogism, and can make the connection. Our existence is justified by these miscreants.

*

Every thinker has a motif even when there is none.

*

Holy places continue to interest me for several reasons. In most cases, they are crafted with a high degree of dexterity, they are impervious against time—

so it seems. But most impressive, they stand unabashedly, housing the sins of the world. How do they claim purity; how can they be holy?

*

Secret: God is not our inquisitor.

*

With the ubiquity and accessibility of salvation, why is hell a concern? Why does humanity still feel morally bankrupt.

*

Suffering has not changed. Neither have our questions. Is there a connection . . . when our questions change, so will our sufferings.

*

I blame language and memory as the system of all sufferings.

&

Vaulted confessions, once held sacred, now transparent, violate the importance of memory. Time always has its way!

&

What is beneath language—this is an anti-thought.

&

If I think this, I cease to exist.

=

The irony remains—language is a system, which allows and prohibits thought.

*

Language does not control my facticity until others recognize it.

*

Science tells us that the Universe is still expanding at the speed of light. What are the implications of this? Where are we in relationship to this phenomena—in 2003 or 3007? Is the Universe expanding at years beyond the one I recognize? When the Universe starts to recede, at what year will we meet its regression, or will humankind regress infinitely beyond numerical expression? Why does this issue bother me so much? Does this truly matter? The illusion that I recognize to be an illusion is time. Time is a narrative, perhaps the only significant narrative. Every facet of human existence and non-existence is referenced in time. To understand this fact is to control time, to step outside of time, to be an active participant of time. As one evaluates his or her existence, deciding whether to continue or to repudiate it, he or she is contemplating the two greatest stories ever told: one that is religious, the other that is scientific. The verdict, I am not too sure . . . but to acquiesce to either one is to say yes to time.

*

Numbers permit us to see the carbon copies of ourselves—God.

*

Numbers are quite intricate, all baring a unification factor.

*

Kierkegaard's problem was no different from Spinoza's problem. Kierkegaard created God in prose. Spinoza created God in numbers.

*

As I noted before, human mortality tries to escape time.

*

I am not a metaphysician.

*

Did Wittgenstein say what everyone else did not care to admit? There are no philosophical problems, only language games; he figured this out in two books. We should not be astonished.

*

Almost a year from today, I vacationed in Hungary; within the past 10 years, councils and leaders declared socialism to carry out the affairs of the country. The effects of post-communism have spurred a search for thought followed by expression. What strikes me as precarious is not the government but the peoples' adaptation to silence. In Hungary, everything is silent. The morning is silent. In between the sidewalk is silence. The sky is silent. St. Stephens— his death was a result of his silence. The canonized statues besieged with rust are silent. Stalin, ghostly memories of Mussolini, German tanks are grounded in silence. Heroes square is silent. What memories are held in Hungary? Next to Northern Africans, Hungarians have the keenest sense of vision. Their eyes narrate microscopic stories of being that is why they are silent. Never to haste after sterile expression, their silence tells all. Verbosity is the crucifix of all silence. I don't blame the French for censuring and monitoring the infiltration of American vocabulary any more than I blame the Hungarians for buffering Magyar from other ethnic acquisitions—primarily due to its complexity, but beneath its syntax is a precise language that communicates exactly what its people feel and think. Silence.

*

I am afraid that the romantic and Slavic tongues will lose their expression. Millions of people will continue to have nothing to say, which is not the same as silence! What will persist is phatic communication. Those lucky enough to learn how to speak will turn to silence, which is not an ethnic tongue. It is an intellectual tongue. Cioran said it best: an intellectual has no nationality. He should also have concluded that an intellectual has no native tongue. His mistake was that he exchanged Romanian for French. I am no linguist, but would you not agree that all language has its limitations. French afforded him a discourse unknown to Romanian language, yet he still discovered limitations. It was through his wrestle with language that he found silence and stopped writing and speaking. The ink from his pen became stale. He became silent—alas he has a voice.

EMPTY TRANSITIONS

On Budapest, Hungary

The city divided into two enveloped me, partly because it was unfamiliar and alien. Perhaps those observations of mine stirred the very feelings I've yearned for since childhood. Hurriedly, folks walk down the streets with their eyes piercing the cobblestone, while the dark wind from their hurriedness concocts memoirs of aged soldiers marching and of repressive regimes.

On God

God and philosophy will date. Wittgenstein, who refused to acknowledge God, once wrote that he could not help seeing every problem "from a religious point of view." Perhaps what emerges here is a refusal to admit the probable. Thinkers recognize the limitations of their own thought, but rarely do they admit to these limitations. Rather, some push folly to success, some turn to narrative writing, and some resign. God is an issue that will always be in question. Imagine a stain so insoluble that no formula or chemical can extricate, then picture God as the stain. God, like language, is everywhere. Even if you choose to extricate God from your mind, you do so making a conscious and fastidious logic premeditated to destroy God. God is at the center of consciousness. I warn you—Dostoyevsky said it best—be aware, be aware. Man lives to satisfy his full capacity that includes his confoundedness with God. A friend of mine questioned my interpretation on Cioran. He said, 'G', you are mistaken, Cioran does not believe in God. My reply is that his anti-God sentiment is what fueled his insomnia. The very fact that he wrestles to extricate himself from God is my proof of his passion for God. The counterpart of philosophies dialectic is partnered with God. Yes, its evil brother!! One banters the other.

Johns Cage

Silence: lectures and writings—1961

Yesterday, which is to say today, because opposites are really non-opposites, a continuous system of degrees rather than absolutes, I read John Cage—dizzy writer and musician. He writes and I write. . . .
I have nothing to say and I am saying it and that is poetry
I have to say poetry and is that nothing and am I saying it I am and I have poetry to say and is that nothing saying it I am nothing and I have poetry to say and that is saying it I then m saying poetry have nothing and it is I and to say What is he saying does it matter, he is saying it too often the functional side of language reminds us of the order of the universe the way things should look I prefer fluid thought uninterrupted by syntax semantics and other such stuff that is the problem with this world you wait for a period and I say no you wait for a comma and i say fuck you you go to tell with your conventions who is john cage where is the author where did john cages quote end and where did the author begin like the computer trying to make sense of the print you are confused you lose your place and its like trying to find waldo in london paris america lose yourself in the picture the words skip over convention you want to the edge is really not an edge it is another flat surface the event horizon will pull you in there are no worries institutions gods to save you rip out this page from the book recite john cage forwards is the same as reciting him backwards your life lived forward is the same lived backwards you would not change a thing if you could do so maybe add a couple more road maps i hope there is no heaven and your disappointment will be your hell

PLATONIC ADVICE ON LOVE AND VIRTUE

Forms Loves Eros.
Or
Loves Forms Eros.

Or
Eros Forms Love.
Who has. . . . gotten it right.

*

Happiness
Please forgive me for my romantic thinking. Perfection:
The scent of a woman!

*

Vanishing
Interesting
Interestin...
Interesti...
Interest...
Interes...
Intere...
Inter...
Inte....
Int...
In...
I...
....

*

MSILE
:0))0:) : O

*

Ciss, Kiss

Creamy, Cold, Claustrophobic Kiss
wavering, winding, wondering, whimpering
slowly, subtly, shortly, soothing, seemingly
forever, feverish, flourishing, faintly
liberating, lively, luring, lying, lips.

ERRANT CONFESSIONS OUT OF CONVULSION

I go mad when I chase after expression. How do I clarify thought? How do I assemble language, a series of fragments and embryonic thoughts? The hardest part of expression is the first words of expression. Whenever I write or speak, I feel violent; this is my curse, my shame, and my exile. Moments of brilliance overwhelm me, but they are only intelligible to me. The veil no longer preserves my incompetence. I am exiled. I am not clear. My request is mute. The circle will look at me with shame. Pretending not to care, I will continue to write, only if for a person, thing, or an idea. Approbation is not necessarily the aim, neither is disapproval. Silence I prefer. Cioran spoke of lucidity as if it were a simple acquisition of thought followed by action. If it were so easy, then I would be the great expatiator, the rhetorical genius. How can he say such things? Remember Antonio Blok, reflecting on the most human parts of his existence, states: what about those who can't believe but want to believe? Lucidity demands more than will and even risky thought—it demands sadism.

On Reading Existential Thought

Nothing is more untenable then reading page for page one's obituary. Nothing brings me greater felicity than to see death patiently masturbating over the future demise of rational thought, the myth of progress. Like a cancer waiting to spread, it waits and is not tired by waiting. Surreptitiously, it conquers until there is nothing left to conquer, similar to a vulture hovering around a dead carcass, cleaving skin away to reveal flesh, existentialism similarly effaces supercilious existence; it makes God a demon. (Existentialism is a wise man's Achilles heel; it is a seekers coat of armor.) There is no qualifying it as a system of thinking or a category of X, Y, Z—it is. Those who classify it, confine it. Existentialism, to the intellectual, the seeker, is the food for nourishment—it is his lover and wife simultaneously. It is not worried about categorical imperatives, forms, syllogisms, excluded middles; these are all counterintuitive. Camus said—All thought starts with suicide and its permissibility. Mathematics, Science, and all other types of reasoning are secondary. What is the relationship between the reader and the discourse?

Too often, and very much the norm, there ceases to exist any grappling with an "X" match with the human condition—just postulations, equations, and theories. The existentialist has no weapons. There is no distance between the human condition and himself; therefore, life bleeds him into a state of paroxysm, beyond all repair. And if you ask existentialists how was their day, they will lament, 'the same as tomorrow'. Today's existentialists are far less irascible and overzealous in their agitation. Existing in a world all their own, they read, write, drink wine and coffee, and are less likely to engage in serious conversation; rather, they speak with the dead. Their personal notes inside their text are the extent of their conversation.

I often ask myself how and when will existentialism die? In recent days, I have been troubled by both ideas. Perhaps existentialism is already dead. If it is dead, it is dead only in theory. It will continue to haunt men, like it did Goethe. But our humanity will blame its death on war, famine, natural resources, God, and so forth. It is really man's attempt to apologize to himself for his supercilious attitude. I do not give humanity too much credit because people will never understand the root of their problems—humanity.

On Tangents

Have Cage and Wittgenstein ever met? I can't think of anyone who has pushed language to submission than Cage and Wittgenstein. I can't think of anyone who has pushed thought further than Cioran.

Chess

Only moments ago, I was stumped for words. There is nothing alarmingly new with that. Instead of drinking coffee, the drink of inspiration, I played chess and realized just how much barbarism chess exudes.

On Not Being Supercilious

Once again, this idea leads to an impasse in my writing. Vaculik wrote, on words, that his attempts at saying anything authentic leads to a dry pen on invisible paper. Perhaps what he is expressing is the inevitable end—writing and thinking leads to itself. The truth is that some of us are better at pretending than others. Out of all of the essays, philosophical and literary, I think Socrates stated what has seemed to be an irrevocable platitude: what differentiates us from God is that we have an interminable yearning of want. Just for a moment, recollect memories of others' praises toward you. Did you resist them? I gather you reluctantly replied, "no." To become God, you have to resist commenting when I, or anyone else, say—What do you think? I should extend the latitude of the comment to say, refuse to offer your opinion even when someone asks you to do so. Still confounded, I am tossing and turning, losing sleep on another idea. . . .

Brief Note on Silence

What has the world against silence? Every morning I enter into a relatively tranquil place, besieged by my own thoughts and redundancies. I even sip the hot, sometimes tepid coffee at the same pace. Enter the mobs with music, with no purpose other than to bring me to the cliff of insanity—I will jump. Heaven, what a wonderful thought? Yes. But there is no more silence, peace, and quiet in heaven than there is in hell.

Reading–Writing

Writing is such an exhausting experience; I can only imagine how readers feel.

The Thinking of a Heterodox

The importance of believing in a purpose and an end governs my thought and actions. It is the string on which I am led to believe that what I am writing eventually makes a contribution toward my own end. Both *purpose* and *end* lead me to believe that between them resides self-deception? Dung has more pragmatic value than any one person of importance. Knowing this, what then delays ignominy, every individual from slitting their wrist? To avoid abstraction lets call "it" hope, purpose, imperatives and anxiety. Take your choice; they are all romantic prayers signifying a future. Be aware Hegel is not dead.

*

Hermeneutics is Pandora's box. There is nothing else to say.

*

Why must I waste time on providing syllogisms? Will you believe me that much more? Am I more credible? My guess is no. Your existence, like mine, is a reconfirmation of what you want to believe. Either way, self-reflection starts and ends with self.

*

My writing is more picturesque. It is both fact and fiction and sometimes neither; it is interesse, vacillating between heaven, hell, and purgatory.

*

I want the world to taste my blood when it boils, my flesh when it stales. Then they ask from whence does this vulgar language emanate? I say from your perverse existence.

*

Foundationalism, if one chooses to *follow*, will ultimately lead to resignation, a state of existence similar to being a Christian, Muslim, and Satanist at once —foundationalsim invites inquisitiveness, followed by possibility!

*

Forever will I teeter with resignation and acceptance. Both are like fine distilled vodkas. When I tire of one, the other awaits. This particular state of existence demands awareness and more vodka.

*

What is achieved by believing? My inability to believe heightens. My heart hardens? My determination to die increases; thus, I live.

*

I no longer close my eyes in prayer.

*

Surrealism is to give in to one's inner fluidity, sense of imperfection, and being.

*

—Andre Breton-1969 Manifestos of surrealism

It is, in fact, difficult to appreciate fairly the various elements present; one may even go so far as to say that it is impossible to appreciate them at a first reading. To you who write, these elements are, on the surface, as strange to you as they are to anyone else, and naturally you are wary of them. Poetically speaking, what strikes you about them above all is their extreme degree of immediate absurdity, the quality of this absurdity, upon closer scrutiny, being to give way to everything admissible, everything legitimate in the world: the disclosure of a certain number of properties and of facts no less objective, in the final analysis, than the others.

EXAMINATIONS IN THE DARK 1–11: CHILDHOOD VISIONS

Examination 1
Ingmar Bergman's Seventh Seal

Some stares carry so much gravity and seriousness that most pressing issues seem trivial. Look at Death's eyes, his mounting tension. Nervousness overwhelms the knight into infinite paralysis. Freed from God, the knight whimpers, if not only for reprieve. God's silence, once proof of his omnipresence, now proves his inexistence.

Naiveté is salvation, the gloss that consumes man's expression the moment Death overshadows his salvation, the stench of fear. Nothing in this world can abate the space between life and death—the first is a truism. There is no escape from velocity, rhetorical argument, or existential cry that deters death. Holy Water or Holy Fire? Truth or a Lie? Neither matters. Hell is neither the absence nor presence of Heaven. Let's say it's the comprehension of nothingness and meaninglessness. There is no case deserving to be solved. The question is: how should one fill the space with which time engenders anxiety and dread—chess for some and good drink for others?

Examination 2
13 year old prostitute in Male

She looks inaccessible—possessed by infinite space—enveloped by time. Her existence is the pendulum of indifference vacillating between nothingness and ennui. It is the state of *interesse*—nothing else matters.

Examination 3
Jesus's Kiss of Betrayal

The kiss of betrayal or innocence, what did Judas think? Christ had never been concerned with honesty. Christ, chided Peter when he drew his sword on the soldier; Lot's wife was condemned for turning to face the city, Adam for being human, the two thieves—one to the left and the other to the right of Christ—one damned, the other venerated, and most of all, Thomas for doubting the resurrection. I might ask, what shall come of us who incessantly question? No one is beyond reproach. The kiss humanizes. Judas is more human than Christ. He marched toward his fate, his suicide—a self-imposed choice —all the more honorable. Christ's suffering was senseless. In principle, I suffer more because of his suffering? Many have suffered before him and the same stands true for the aftermath. Judas's kiss reminds me that my suffering, salvation, heaven, and hell are my own—most of all my humanity.

Examination 4
Returning to Café I use to Frequent

Leaving a space that you once occupied, only to return to find it occupied is disconcerting. The space does not change. It can't, and I am not sure why. I have not even considered the people amid the now occupied space. My reaction confirms how man has more in common with a ravage-ridden four-legged animal than the sophisticated chimp he says he is.

Examination 5
A picture of Silence

I have noticed the world is not so quiet in the way I have come to know it— in fact, it appears strident and cluttered. The coffee shop is where I do most of my writing, praying, meditating, and synthesizing. Lucidity is most often confronted in the bar—a conduit to surrealism. Spirited conversation coupled with martinis makes life tolerable. It makes up for those immature encounters one has with an unexpected stranger, or an involuntarily conversation one hears on public transportation. My point is there are very few places on earth where other animals have not made the once sacred, vile. I loathe my existence for this very point. My birth was vile; my birth picture shows a petulant ridden face. A babe that wanted to die as soon as he was birthed—it was not my choice in the matter. My next point, forgive me for my insolent behavior.

Examination 6
A picture of Jesus' Crucifix

People just don't die; they commit suicide. At one point in their life, they mutter an indecipherable wish in their sleep begging for their end. Life's delayed response then renders them their wish. Jesus committed suicide. I dare you to say it. . . . Life is suicide—its all suicide, some suicides are subject to religious naiveté and pious conviction, while others out of pure exhaustion.

Examination 7
Ingmar Bergman's Wild Strawberries

Listen to the sound of the clock ticking. Do you hear it reverberating throughout your eardrum? Hear the thickness of its echo, its parabolic movement, its linear progression, tirelessly possessed as to reach an end. That is your life my friend, eager to leave you, ready to end; it has no remorse, trapped in your gangrene body, ready to leave in order to become a tree.

Examination 8
On Not Wanting to Live

Of the most fatiguing feelings in everyday experience is listening. Imagine those public servants of God, who attentively listen to the most debauched and reckless of sins. Their ears and hearts are heavy. Who listens to them— God? Instinctively, my reply is "no," as I find no presence of God in this world beyond what I have rehearsed in grammar school. Mankind's very preoccupation with this idea illustrates an interminable dependence, even a blind dependence. Nothing can illuminate the morose color of existence. The question we must ask ourselves is how long can we endure, persevere the perils of our own self-inflicted existence? I am certain of nothing except death. My preparation for death determines my *existenz*. Lack of preparation, I believe, ensues a voluptuous torture—mental flagellations of the greatest degree. God's inwardness and solipsism is an inward energy and gravity, stretching the limits of the physical and mental fibers of *existenz*. Even if God is sophomoric, I have no choice but to recognize him, even if my recognition is that of contempt and acrimony.

Examination 9
A Picture of World Leaders

I am not convinced by words, for they are quickly and easily written, learned, and applied. The man instilling credibility and stock in them beware. One man's will does not speak for all; his will is a product that is forced and forged in the minds of those whose existence depended on such drivel.

Examination 10
A Picture of Camus

Least endurable and most proper is a brilliantly failed mind. A mind such as the one I'm thinking about never looks for approbation, neither does it practice servitude—its errors are its own, and its successes follow suit. Pursuits, ideals, and objectives are a matter of time fillers. The mind does not care about them. It understands their value and function and chooses to bother with them at its leisure.

Examination 11
A Beautiful Woman

Absolutely stunning—her face! Against all social sensibilities, I continue to stare and stare. Our eyes met and she knew that my stares were not insidious —just eyes that had stumbled upon Beauty.

ANATHEMAS AND SELF-DECEPTION

Thoughts

Death was never so near than in the Enlightenment. A day or so ago, soaking in the bath, I surmised the evolution of thought, progress, the emergence of a new paradigm. One that abnegates old values and achieves human authenticity has always and will continue to remain allusive—Why? Boredom is as humanly biological as the human need to reproduce.

Titleness

Why have we become obsessed with titles? Titles to papers, titles to films, titles of achievements, and Titles. A few years ago, a professor mentioned to me, "There is no title on this paper. There is nothing. What can I do with this?" Immediately, my reply—"To what seriousness does a title impose on a work?" On another occasion he asked, "Why do you write for yourself?"

Causes of Malaise

1. The unbearable lightness of being
2. Vertigo
3. History
4. Quotidian
5. Forgetting of Being
6. Wisdom of uncertainty
7. Antithesis
8. Ennui
9. Volition

Causes of Insomnia

Few conditions in life summon the gravity of my existence more than insomnia; and for that, my mind lay between *being* and *non-being,* enervating my existence, while souring the need to be 'X.' I have some reservation in declaring both *being* and *non-being* as states of existence since they are projections of. . . .

On Marriage

Marriage = indivisibility of psychosis; negation; hollowness; privation of self. Marriage usurps psuedonimity from life, not out of spite but out of a lack of interest, longing for death—the penultimate progression into ego-privation. In that regard, one returns to a state *of*. While there are many ways to do so, I only know of two.

Cataclysms

I write to counteract the quotidian of my existence. Each thought is a nail in my coffin that I dare not dislodge. With rapid furry, I incessantly think thought after thought. Some are lucky enough to escape this activity—but it is my fate. I stand in front of you bloody and bowed, not willing to defend myself. My birth was my sentencing—cursing it does me no good; I am still guilty.

Apologies

I have apologized for wrong-doings I never committed. Since my birth bares misfortune to others, an apology is owed to all.

On Suffering

There is no pre-determined suffering beyond that which germinates from egoism, but let's play the suffering game. Tell me, what is gained and lost from believing in such drivel? Reprieve? Amnesty? Acquittal? From what—your self? Let us praise Eve for original sin, the Fallen Angels for self-transcendence, Goethe for his social intercourse with the Mephistopheles. Call it what you will, our egos desire approbation to facilitate our drunken illusions. Those who suffer the most expect the most—it is all too simple.

On Temerity

Tuesday, April 13, 2004, resignation stirred my intentions and became History, but yet I am an observer, no longer a participant. The fabric of my thought torn asunder, never uttered again. History and ambition, the measure of progress recedes into Heraclites River. This day, the mirror reflects what it perceives. I sit, remain seated, hoping for a cup of coffee.

On Reflection

Depthless gazes seldom bare a reflection; hence, the gaze becomes that more insightfully diminutive—vestiges of the infinite moment remains.

Contingency

When all else fails, drink coffee.

—E.M. CIORAN: SOME THOUGHTS

Every project is a camouflaged slavery- Cioran (1971) p.175.

*

I'd rather offer my life as a sacrifice than be necessary to anything. Cioran (1991) p.118.

*

Each concession we make is accompanied by an inner diminution of which we are not immediately conscious. Cioran (1971) p.78.

*

Meaning is conceivable only in a finite world where one can reach something, where there are limits to stop our regression, clear points of reference, where history moves toward a goal envisioned by the theory of progress. Cioran (1992) p.98.

*

To be weary of what you have desired but even of what you *could* have desired! Indeed, of any possible desire. Cioran (1971) p. 97.

*

One is and remains a slave as one is not *cured* of hoping. Cioran (1971) p.102.

*

Since there is no salvation either in existence or in nothingness, let this world with its eternal laws be smashed into pieces. Cioran (1992) p.28.

On Suffering

Imagine the temperature at which the blood percolates when one commits an act of suicide, only to find that Hades is not interested in his appeal. One can never summon Hades! A lofty thought—A suicidal calmness veils what otherwise might be considered a capricious lassitude.

*

If time does not exist, then what is to be said about my suffering?

*

No thought is truer than the constancy of my happiness, all contingent on the forwardness of death, and that every day my existence is proclaimed. I am one day closer to death.

*

Socrates' life—a contagion to all.

*

To extricate oneself from privations—one must sacrifice all that is human to be an ascetic. Still, there is no guarantee; the lease hold continues.

*

It is time to go to Fiji.

*

Perhaps the lassitude of my existence is recognizing that every enunciation and thought extricates me from nothing.

*

Pleasure consists not in acquiring and enjoying but not desiring—If wisdom is defined as opposition to Desire, it is because wisdom is concerned to make us superior to the ordinary disappointments as well as to the dramatic ones, inseparable, on either count, from the phenomenon of desiring, expecting, hoping.

*

Suffering reminds me of my ineptness and mortality.

*

Words are associations of associations—my existence seems to follow suit.

*

I happily await the day when there is nothing more to speak about.

*

The last thought written on this page took place two months ago. Two months later, I have nothing to say, a fool's life. I continue to ask myself when shall I lay to rest my confession? Have I more to say that has not yet been declared? Surely not.

*

I greet everyone that enters my place of rest with beer, martini, or cigar. How can I otherwise justify hospitality?

*

Surely the day will come that I have been longing for some time. Only then, I will beg for it to go away. Time is on time's side.

*

How fortunate if thou should learn the benefits of contentment.

*

Rarely has M.A. name been spoken. Perhaps, it is better that way!

*

Enough time has passed and space filled, life mimicked, books read/surveyed that my own thoughts seem fraudulent and mere apparitions of those I have admired.

*

The greats wrote out of compulsion. What happens when there is no compulsion in one's life—one then returns to their original state? I look forward to that day.

*

My goal is the journey—I have begun. The choice that confronts me is how far l go. I know I am traveling all the time but where?

*

Fyodor's lunacy is no different than ours. An old colleague of mine revealed a Marxist truism. One works to work. Camus had a love–hate relationship with work—perhaps the true death of an intellectual.

*

The first question asked of me in the year 2005 was How was your New Year? To that I replied, the same as the year to come.

*

Celebration, a constant reminder of how uninspired and socially retarded/delinquent one is in regard to others. Early in life, one is given a party. Later in life, one has to throw a party for oneself.

*

The language of celebration is a quest to extricate oneself from time. Judaic mythology reminds us, time is not faithful to none only to itself.

*

The phraseology—passing time.

*

All intellectualism and seemingly anti-intellectualism are similar. They echo escapism.

*

Those that find comfort in academic learning, remembering, and reciting are no different from their religious counterparts—its all ideology. We all believe in something, someone, or some thought; if one could find a difference, it is in the degree of *lunacy*.

*

I just recalled some thoughts on Schopenhauer and Emerson. There is a moment in everyone's education in which they have to take a stand, make a claim, and practice what seems to be their own philosophy.

*

My fear is that I become so book learned that I stop thinking.

*

Yesterday, a thought prompted a revelation that I would like to share. I have no problems withdrawing from day-to-day interaction, enjoying life at my pace. However, what makes life worthwhile, I think, is doing.... When one no longer does, then one questions.

*

Language muddies everything, penetrates the mind, becomes the mind, and is the mind.

*

Discourse, no matter how effective, ineffective, or life affirming, must begin with a willingness by the agent(s) who seek change. I may be of a minority who believe ideology is neutral; it is always the people seeking change that will and wield the discourse propitious.

*

Someone once asked, replace God and what do you have? My reply: God.

*

The absurd is the wincing and the continuous rubbing of one's eye, only to find there is no eyelash.

*

Dialogue promises but never comforts.

On Hysteria

Lunacy derives from the vulturistic apparitions that pose as a reminder that freedom is not a choice—I am free. I can never choose my freedom; by virtue of my birth, I am free. At the age of 18 I was born and do not quite recollect an existence before that point. I felt freedom, its dolefulness and its natural gravity toward Hades. I never fought back, simply immuring Hades with all my being.

*

Language attenuates freedom, but it does not bring about resolve. Freedom is freedom; there is nothing beyond freedom. The prison I call freedom has invisible walls, and only if we knew how suffocating these walls really were would we all take our lives into our own hands—but it is always too late to kill oneself. And it is not death, hysteria, or lunacy that one seeks to extricate one's self from. I might add that these conditions are all symptoms of a voluptuous belief in a utopia and a history of progress. Progress is the discourse of West, a timeline to most Westerners. And yet, with each waking moment, my physical being recedes from west to east. I am none the more wiser or smarter. I am aware. . . . I see the train coming, and I can't move—this is freedom.

On Travel

There is A s-p-a-c-e for everyone, find it.

An Extended Holiday to Ireland

Friendship, Hospitality, and Pride from the countrymen of Ireland are unrivaled. 16-3-05, a celebration of the highest order took place at the old Joyce restaurant. Plates of Guinness stew and spirit after spirit of mature spiced Jamison cured our doleful disposition, while wooden clogs reverberated against the creaky floor and up the wall, creating silhouettes from aged lighting. Filled with drink and meal, we tried our tongues at old Irish folk tunes. Never once did it cross our minds that our tongues were not Gaelic, but the cadence was easily followed and was well received by the natives. We cheered and cheered until the moon decided to take five, only to realize that our time was waning, too. The four of us understood time and did not try to preserve it. Like the torrents of Guinness and Jamison we drank, we enjoyed it for what is was, not what it could be. Time was neither slow nor fast. No one eulogized the moment; it was just a moment understood. We never spoke of it again. Never once was I tempted to record these moments, though easy enough if I were to preserve it. Let me do so, leaving to chance the forgotten memories of the warm hobbitian friendship and choleric conversations of Joyce, Jameson's distillation process, the wonderment of the Cliffs of Morria, and the Temple Bar. We were strangers, friends, and strangers again.

Some thoughts of Elsewhere

How much of our existence is imaginary and fictive? What then are we to make of the self? Every concession to any self is nothing short than pathological egoism.

*

Humankind is an eternal contagion—there is no rhetorical flourish on words.

*

It is exactly the 'Other' that I retreat from. There earnest ignorance couched as wisdom is cumbersome. They request conversation, hoping that you can appeal to their priggishness; I listen to them as they insult me unwittingly. Truly, this is the only redeeming value of communication—I am just as stupid as you are, and we are comrades.

*

My ecstasy—my last words. Sartre's last words, reportedly, find God. Goethes's last words, reportedly, 'The Cross is the most hideous image on the earth; more light!

*

My last words will never be my own; they will always be misinterpreted.

*

In most ways, writing has become more difficult than I imagined because I no longer have an audience. When one has something to say, there is never an audience, and I imagine the opposite is true.

*

What is your fate—to have accomplished nothing and to die overworked; this is true for the most accomplished and the least accomplished.

*

Everyone believes in something—be it God or Nothingness. Camus's characters in the Possessed are immured in such dissidence.

*

When I see myself aging in thought, I retreat to Rossenhale; my Pierre . . . I exclaim . . . my Govinda. . . . Lost innocence—there it is given without one's request, and it is taken away without one's asking. We go to such lengths—why? To become again what we were before we were.

*

Compassion is the most meaningful act.

*

The same languid clouds I saw in Switzerland hovered over me in Washington —the silence I felt in Hungary spoke to me in Ireland. Etc.

*

How many fictions must one read and hear in order to take action? Indolence is the same as indifference, but not quietism and resignation.

*

A quite disturbing event occurred this past Tuesday. I walked into a room filled with beautiful women—I wanted to die, but continued...

*

The ultimate martyrdom and alienation is marriage.

*

We are all good for one conversation.

*

Mazes of buildings prefigure day-to-day life; for most, the maze is a preposterous enigma, routine drivel at best. Yesterday, I entered the maze, aghast at what appeared to be a woman with a tail, a man with whiskers, and others with claws, jockeying for position.

*

City eyes are telling. One never exists until another engages them for better or for worse. This is why our proximity to windows is crucial.

*

I am a coward because I beckon death. Wonder about those who masturbate about death; they are just as guilty as those who hide in their fictions.

*

Dead people are more interesting than the living—no one beckons them they just are.

*

My allegiance to a God is conceptual. I know nothing other than concepts— I am a concept.

*

Quite honestly, I am writing for myself.

*

Certitude, Promise, and Hope are nothing but manifestations of the Will.

*

Several articles have been published to my credit, but nothing has changed. After completing my graduate studies, nothing has changed. . . . This honest cycle continues. The drivel of it all.

*

I am sitting in a coffee shop, 8:03 p.m., EST—a man immures himself with a fifth cup of coffee.

*

What to play, how to deceive, and what theoretical framework to utilize are sums of the 21st century.

*

Physical ineptness, a gentle reminder that one is aging—don't loathe. Aging is freedom, a divorce from conventions, a return to childhood.

*

I think about T.P. from time-to-time. He seems rather irascible, that's my best surmise. My thoughts are with you, friend.

*

Age also makes one less tolerant, more contentious, less seduced by conversation and platitudes.

*

Absurdity shows itself in the Fall.

*

A homeless man asked for small change. I continued to walk. He said, "Thank you."

*

Criticism is futile: One should aim not to understand criticism, but to understand oneself.

*

I loathe my university training. To make up for it, I write and publish, everything short of hiding in a cave; that is my insecurity.

*

We talked—her paltry lips touched mine. This is a true intellectual exchange.

*

Thinking and doing both have limits.

*

Walking through the transparent maze, the last idea in mind is to exit. The act of extricating oneself from the maze is tantamount to a case of sever megalomania.

*

Is there a maze?

*

Failure seems to be my only friend.

*

Not a thought-provoking thought runs through this place.

*

[X] never saw me; she noticed that I am transparent amidst crowd.

*

For Stravrogin, abstention of faith verifies his faith.

*

Linguistic purity hides in silence.

*

A double malt Jamison, please.

*

What is admirable about Wittgenstein is that he said what was needed in one book and that was sufficient. Verbosity in the 21st century signifies stupidity, not profundity.

*

Accomplishment begets insanity, the oracle said.

*

Behind every smile looms depression.

*

What pernicious knowledge does the Stoic keep to himself—that self-actualization leads to interminable thoughts of one's death? Waiting for one's death, like water vapor escaping the tea kettle, so it is with life inevitably exiting the corpse.

Chapter Two

The 'B' Book: Sanguine Thoughts for a Hapless World

SOME THOUGHTS ON FUTILITY, ENNUI, QUOTIDIAN, AND CONSCIOUSNESS

The forecast for the next five days promises to be warm. I suggested to my wife maybe I should water the flowers. Yes, I will do that today.

*

There is no greater obstacle to deliverance than the need for failure.

*

No object is worth being desired. What is worth desiring?

*

Yesterday, to be exact, by what was an unfortunate meeting at "A", I met "H", who has not changed, and I do not ever expect people like him to change. The first question he asked was "Did you buy **** To him, I replied, "No." He told me he bought 'X' Continuing to probe, he asked "Aren't you tired of school, having already graduated?" My reply, somewhat incensed, was "No!!!" He stared at me with vacuous eyes, and I saw emptiness, but that brief moment of absurdity passed away. We drank and eulogized the night.

*

At the intersection of every thought is awareness, even if it is unintentional.

*

A useless passion, to desire God. Speech reminds us of this drivel.

*

There was a time before the Renaissance when God was in prayer's reach; since the Renaissance, a customary practice is to paint God and idolize God. We have lost all concept of God; God is forever lost in an ineffable simulacra.

*

Western thinkers revel in negation—thesis/antithesis/binary opposites/ dialectics, etc. Not too much has changed after Aristotle.

*

Cessation—there was a point at which this word made sense. Sharing in our problem with Alienation is that language is overly optimistic. Language itself is a product of hope and progress, but English is inept—it lacks feeling and specificity. Yet, to English's credit, it has more adjectives than any other language.

*

I read the greats with an understanding that their stupor impinges at a far greater depth than mine, but I read to understand myself rather than others.

*

Last night I died; today I live—I commence the rest of my life.

*

Freedom is lamentation without shame or fear of saving face.

*

My life has been one that understands responsibility; thus, diffidence is an organic response to situations requiring responsibility.

*

A perfect marriage is a wife without voice and a husband without ears.

*

I entered the church and protested to the saints. "The more one has suffered, the less one demands. To protest is a sign one has not really suffered." Jostled, they prayed for me.

*

From the moment we are born, we become mortal, take a number, and loathe. No one is so fortunate as to extricate him- or herself from the situation. We are left to voluptuous devices that only enervate the "situation." Mortality, once recognized, is traumatizing, a sick joke played by God. History is nothing but humankind's dissidence against God, but God never shows His face, so dissidence appears to be at best infinite drivel. Picture a baby crying in the dark only to find no caretakers.

*

Few will admit to this: mortality and stupor are solipsistic reminders of our fragility. Human intelligence resorts to procreation in hopes to return the favor to God. God destroys, and humankind creates. I have no illusions who will champion this duel.

*

I do not believe in syllogistic thesis and antithesis—both are part of our debacle and hackneyed "situation."

*

The other day I read an article suggesting that both of Wittgenstein's books were saying the same thing—nothing.

*

Writing is a matter of forgetting and the reader remembering.

*

Intentions are more pernicious than actions.

*

Beneath every smile is venom.

*

Nothing is ever so sobering as marriage—there is no chaser.

*

A day of reckoning awaits everyone, when life decides it is time for us to remember rather than forget. I am horrified by this day, call it judgment day. Even as I speak, my being is suffering from its inability to forget—I must not petition!

*

I made a fool out of myself the other day. What else is new?

*

The unimportance of being born.

*

.... Separated by more than....

*

Death has never been so close than at the beginning of one's life.

*

My birthday is soon to arrive. Once again I am reminded of the drivel of my existence—what a mockery.

*

How many times must I die?

*

The French language is difficult because I do not love it; I will have a hand at Rumanian.

*

As of late, I have been overtaken by work, something I am not used to. Without reprieve, my body weakens and falls dormant in slumber while my eyes are wide awake—my understanding of insomnia. I fight with my insomnia and nausea; my petulance is a sign of revolt. I am none the more closer to resignation than yesterday.

*

Coffee, an infatuation of mine, is now a curse of necessity.

*

Society will eventually reach terminal velocity; kinetic energy reaches a point of apex, then. . . .

*

There is nothing to say of any consequence to anyone—my tongue is indifferent.

*

Exile has always been the last means of deliverance—inevitable and invariable, a constancy of an intellectual.

*

In my happier days, I carried a cylinder of cyanide to deliver me. Unfortunately, my fate is immortality.

*

Several weeks have passed, and Rumania still bothers me!

*

Here's a thought — at what point in Hell is God inaccessible — I now remember He is no further away from me than I from Him.

*

I stand before this image of Thy face, my God, and while I look upon it with the eyes of sense, I strive with my inner eyes to behold the truth which is figured forth in this picture ... (Cusa, 1960, p.45).

*

To laugh at fiction is to laugh at ourselves. Fiction is the only mirror.

*

I smell the stench of my grave.... I loathe the worms. My work has only been understood as I enumerate abstractions of existence. How does one talk about existence? One drinks its vomit.

*

A smile is just as pernicious as a frown.

*

Some flowers threatened to bloom, and I prayed for them; the next morning I was mistaken, the flowers were weeds.

*

Most interesting about humans is ambition, so it seems the same with all creatures. But ambition is futility, doing without thinking. Other animals do not have a choice. How lucky are they?

*

Ghastly! I looked amid the metro and saw consternated expressions all around me. Were they reading Cioran, Camus, Hume, Sartre? No, they were reading the newspaper. Instant drivel.

*

I have taken up the language of French.

*

Tunis awaits me!

*

I live in a world filled with I pods, and that scares me.

*

Chapter Two

A thought just entered my mind. What I am writing could be my own fate or, as my American idiom suggests, my wish list. Imagine me granted with every expression written thus far.

*

Once again, I live a lie. I walk into the academy besieged by four walls of hypocrisy. Before speaking, I have to ask myself, will this lecture abet in the financial security of my audience? If not, then why broach the issue?

*

How can anyone evince any evidence of God ?

*

Thought never evades nor supercede mythos and cultural tradition.

*

Consciousness of is feeling the drivel of one's existence second by second.

*

Most works that I have found worth remembering were the works of authors that understood resignation.

*

Literary arrogance is the writing when there is nothing more to write.

*

I have been shown the animal that I can become. I have been given everything that I have decided to pursue. Temptation for me is striving for that which I never committed. Today, for example, I redeemed a ticket for a free drink of my choice. I opted for a small coffee. Aghast, the gentleman replied—why not a large? Are your sure? Next year about this time, if life still has me in good favor, I will buy my XXX. In the deep recesses of my mind, I am cognizant of D.H. Lawrence.

*

Isak Borg reminded me that I am no different than the next person, although I differ in my mannerisms. Some are just more pretentious than others.

*

The question is not "who is my maker?" That brings little to no consternation; neither does the question "What becomes of me when I cease to be?" My morosity derives from creation—the unpardonable sin. It makes sense that dissidence was absent from Christ's voice—this is what makes Him human. How the Gnostics bastardize His life—praying for His forgiveness to gain eternal beautitude. One life is enough! Why would one seek immortality! What a sallow logic! It is Christ's death that I see as important. Death was his only reprieve. And we should be happy that He died; his birth is another issue for which we should weep.

*

Throughout the history of Christianity, one always reads and hears of some vessel of Christ protesting for Christ; Christ rarely ever cared to protest on His own behalf. He never took up His own sword. He was a person that wanted to be a human. It is we who are guilty of His birth and death. We made Him an idol to tear Him down!! He never wanted to be God or all that we have made Him to be.

*

Yes, we all will have our hand at Christ. By default, we will become something that we are not. Our fate will share semblance with Socrates, Kierkegaard, Gandhi, and others. There is no protest; our persecutors have no ears.

*

The belief in fiction is the lifeline of human rationality and irrationality—we are all naïve magicians.

*

Literature and philosophy are almost always tutorial to those who understand their aim; the purpose of literature and philosophy is that by reading them we understand ourselves. Never has the purpose crossed my mind to read to understand Nietzsche, Camus, Unamuno, and others to better understand the person.

*

Beckett had much to say about ennui—how fortunate am I to have crossed the absurdist. Perhaps I will visit his grave someday!

*

I wonder if Socrates understood the perverseness of his discourse; maybe he didn't, which was his punishment. Abjuring one's boredom for consciousness is never advisable—his death was honorable.

*

When Camus intimated living is never easy . . . I have to believe he was referring to the act of waiting for one's death.

*

If you ruminate what occupies another person's mind, my reply is nothing but space and the thought of filling space.

*

Are you bored, one asked? Immediately, the gentleman replied, "We all are."

*

To give one's life is to recognize life's insignificance.

*

Some mask their boredom in war, adventure, sport, travel, and writing. Every activity that takes us from our original state is boredom. What eventually threatens human existence is not existence itself, but boredom.

*

Each moment I am stricken with consciousness, which causes my inner body to torpidly palpate.

*

I know there is nothing beyond my own inwardness, and at times I dupe myself into thinking otherwise. Age has become my only friend, and I have been able die day by day without faith.

*

My nephew asked me an encouraging question about time—If we can see into the past; why not into the future?

*

There is nothing truer that we all take our lives too late.

*

In several of my past declarations of death, I have described why humans seek relationships with others. And while consternation may satisfy the sociologist and psychologist, one has to think how much ennui plays a role in our actions and in-actions.

*

I once thought gravity was the final arbiter of destruction—it comes none the closer to the effects of ennui. That is, what starts with ennui also ends with ennui.

*

Today amid my students, I labeled myself stupid. I confessed. Immediately an insidious expression of bewilderment penetrated their cheerful disposition. Silence.

*

Authenticity and honesty are conceptually different but are always positioned as the same.

*

Say it's not so—regeneration!

*

One is always a prostitute—unfortunately, my price is not high.

*

Even Nietzsche condemned his own exile, venturing down from the mountains, to feel all the more isolated among the statesmen. For the exiled, there is no recourse to speak about day-to-day affairs. The quotidian of life is obvious, and the feeling of repetition is too superfluous to stomach.

*

The work of a prostitute is the only honest profession.

*

In my younger days, rejection was a sign of incompetence. Today, it is a languid reminder of my self-acclaimed alienation; if it were not for my incompetence, I would suffocate in my own vomit.

*

The other day I met my maker.

*

Redundancy has always been the delicacy of choice for humankind.

*

To read is serious labor—something that now takes a type of effort. Serious reading is to commit a type of voluntary suicide—hoping that one is immediately cleansed by the words of someone else. How many times have I said there is no salvation, not even from ourselves.

*

It was Truffaut who compared a woman's legs to the arrows on a compass, extending to the outward realm of the universe, giving it balance and grace.

Oh, how much I appreciate enveloping myself in blissful moments of fantasy. Fleeting fantasies . . . We must not make them real or we feel the moral imperative and condemnation of our interloper.

Wittingly, even those aware of boredom succumb to it—it waits as the universe does, never tires by waiting. Even if man is nothing but his endeavors, he eventually runs out of plans.

After our primordial needs are satiated are we then human?

*

Though today repeated yesterday and the day before, I continue to live in duplicity. Thus, I believe today is different from the next.

Hegel like Darwin was correct in his theory of an evolution—but can we discern what good has germinated from a social/physiological evolution?

*

An encouraging thought—today I read that the play *Crime and Punishment* was for viewing at the local black box theater!

*

How easy it is to become enraptured in the quotidian of life—how difficult it is become a recluse.

*

An uneased lady expressed what the world was like before I was born. To that, I replied it was far better than it is today. I find it rather mysterious, somewhat a waste of thought to bother one's self over such issues. It is further proof that we are a virulent virus. History is replete with serious and casual examples of our virulent lineage, which is no different than a shrub or insect.

*

Humans are weeds of destruction!!

*

Recognizing that one has to breathe is hard enough, and to remind one's self of this act is just as cumbersome. Upon my last gasp of air, I will rejoice. How easy it is fantasize about one's death!

*

I have not one flinching doubt that Camus found what he searched for; this is why his death lacks anonymity.

*

With each concession and thought committed to paper, my words become hackneyed without passion.

*

How safe does this sound—Dans certaines situations repondre: rien.

*

When one stumbles upon Beauty it is like having the wind taken out of their soul—one becomes humble, a gracious observer, and is appreciative of sight. And if the eyes become overwhelmed, the heart percolates all the more.

*

All thought and actions lead to an impasse, a truism that has marred all civilizations. How else is one to explain humankind's characteristics of ennui and priggishness. At the end of history, what is left but the mirror of ignominy? Judgment day. Never is it presumptuous to say suicide—judging whether or not life is worth living is the only question of significance.

*

I patiently await the arrival of Cioran's notebooks. His loose writings and mental exercises in torpidity, suicide, and disengagement encourages me to. . . .

*

When one has nothing to read, one writes; and when one has nothing to write, one reads.

*

In America, it is easy to feel uninspired, detach, float, commit suicide, lose footing, and lose definition because there are only distant memories, fragments, and scents of a self.

*

Who prays for God's speed? If he is made in our own image, does he not suffer as we do? Is he not burdened by those 8 million and counting prayer mongers? Who among us can offer solace to him?

*

Human expression, creation, is the panacea for suicide. When there is nothing left to say, one always kills oneself or waits for one's death

*

How can anyone not fall in love with utopianism—we share this love affair with our maker.

*

Occupied by my death, I run away from it by my love of sunshine and coffee.

*

In my middle years, words have become an academician's exercise in deceit. Ambiguity is my preferred tongue. There are times I wish to engage, but that desire is whimsical and is transient at best.

*

Methods and exercises of the ascetic wane in contemporary civilization. In their place, the moderns gleefully offer possibility, in the quantity of "X." Quite ingenious, if I say so myself, for the quantity is mysterious, illusive, has no method of instruction, and most important is labor free.

*

The English language has a way of enticing the imagination to mindless activity; thus, I am writing this and you are reading this.

*

Recognition is the most virulent of all vices.

*

The act of living is always confused with the love of life.

*

Thinking and writing is a cyclical process, like erasing what one has written time and time again.

*

Nothing . . . is the only reply.

*

Today I prayed for Christ and the people who demand so much of him. Let him rest in peace, for he is no longer an exalted savior of men—a heterodox, yes, but failed and forgotten.

*

If there was a modicum of good and reason in this world, it was buried some time ago.

*

Spiritual insomnia is to blame for my mind's restlessness. Today, I plan a holiday and cannot seem to find a favorable destination; this troubles me more than anything. Minds wander away, this is true, and with adequate nurturing, they do return. Yet, my mind shows no reason or interest in returning.

*

Between Hesse and Cioran, I feel lost.

*

If one lives long enough and is unfortunate to see the interminable path that is the quotidian of existence, from that point on one begins to live and living is never caprice.

*

My mind wanders to Turkey, the well-being of Terrance, and how much I really do owe him.

*

On History and Utopia, Cioran wrote about the mental pangs endured from acquiring a new tongue. That in my mind is easier than leaving one's native homeland. While the intellectual has no homeland, s/he is nostalgic and internally laments for the familiar. Plants also lament for familiar soil; the intellectual is no different in certain respects.

*

There are no philosophical problems, how true, how mindless, a reminder of humankind's chicanery.

*

What has the world against accidents, chance, unknown quantities, we are all accidents ?

Chapter Three

The 'C' Book: Thoughts on Bergman, Unamuno, and Camus

THOUGHTS ON INGMAR BERGMAN (1957): THE SEVENTH SEAL

Death: And you don't want to die
Knight: Yes, I do.
Death: What are you waiting for?
Knight: I want knowledge.
Death: You want guarantees.

After consciousness, our fundamental attunement is predicated on the empty fullness lamented by the knight. Yes! Life is a game of mutable dice, a chicanery, an earnest pursuit without direction or guarantee of salvation. William James (1977) and Blaise Pascal found an exit out of this labyrinth that eventually lead us into another labyrinth? If Man chooses to turn his back altogether on God and the future, no one can prevent him; no one can show beyond reasonable doubt that he is mistaken. If Man thinks otherwise and acts as he thinks best, I do not see that any one can prove that he is mistaken. We do not certainly know whether there is any right one. What must we do: "Be strong and of a good courage" (James, 1977, p. 735). Act for the best, hope for the best, and take what comes. If death ends all, we cannot meet death better. There is no greater decision we can make; all else is a romantic cry for salvation, to awaken one's self from the horrid dream which is no dream at all. How brave is Mr. James.

THOUGHTS ON MIGUEL DE UNAMUNO (1954)

The exact date is not so clear, but how I felt is memorable. We Americans often say, when lightning strikes, bottle it! Dare I say that is exactly what I did that day when I read Unamuno for the first time? Unamuno was more than a Spaniard, philosopher, activist, moralist, or artist; he was a maligned seeker that lit dark spaces by whispering truths into the void. From Unamuno, I felt the great contradiction of my existence, a sense of irony, similar to the freedom one has in a straight jacket. A stranger to me, Unamuno lamented—"I am a man; no other man do I deem stranger." Strangeness and contradiction are seeds of human existence, my existence, that which I am incapable of making intelligible. Reading Unamuno, one comes to the realization that Man is an end to himself, nothing else, and so it is that what he romanticizes and dreams about reveals the same end as well. There are moments when one asks in earnest why can't I kill consciousness? The reply is simple—life has seduced any modicum of courage left. James (1977) priggishly urged, Believe, and that belief will provide the courage one needs to live. But what benefit and gain does one have by living in contradiction, knowing there is no exit but by suicide; and even then there is no guarantee? Seekers such as Unamuno, Cioran, and Hesse are no strangers to the truth. Their message is simple and direct—the most tragic problem with existence is the irreconcilable necessities of the heart and the will and the space in between.

ERRANT THOUGHTS ON ALBERT CAMUS

Jean-Paul Sartre, Fyodor Dostoevsky, Friedrich Nietzsche, Ingmar Bergman, and others postulated about the marvelous argument—If God exists, then . . . , a bastardization of Pascal! Does thought, left to its own devices, indulge in nothingness, seduce itself in more naiveté, or cannibalize once it reaches an impasse? Fatigued minds, minds of the desert and sun are product of a hapless optimism, a historical necessity. Camus has been labeled a failed philosopher, or even worse an imposter; some have even paralleled him to Don Juan. Perhaps he is best known for the highly regarded novel *The Stranger* (1946) and least known for his precarious death and confession, *The Myth of Sisyphus* (1955). Above all, Camus was a gentle soul, maligned by politics, quixotism, and hapless events of his time.

Chapter Four

The 'D' Book:
Ennui, Quotidian, and Utopianism

QUOTIDIAN, ENNUI, AND THE AMERICAN: A POSTSCRIPT

We as Americans have no Cesar but have managed to conjure a hologram of one—the least resistant mode of seduction toward utopianism. With unflinching obedience, we have managed to live in accord with the inner promptings of Cesar—cloaking him with precious medals and fabrics, feeding him with exotic spices, and constructing elaborate monuments in his honor. What powers and mystique does he possess—and what injected acquiescing cocktail impinges our being: Quixotic, madness, ennui, longing, amnesia, or seduction? Quixotism is brief, Emile Cioran (1974) warned, but have we been duped into believing our own dictum and catechism—"it's never too late"—tantamount to immortality? We are forever zombies, anesthetized to the real. The ongoings and affairs of the world remain a dead language, without translation. As we are burgeoned from blood, fire, ash, and interminable violence, how are we to identify with the "Other?"

A TRIBUTE TO EMILE CIORAN:
UNPUBLISHED ESSAY 2006–2007 CONTINUED

Ennui, Quotidian, Seductive, Stupidity:
Continued Thoughts on Narrative Episteme

Cioran was right! Human beings have been seduced by technology, and this fetish has become increasingly primal and cognitively numbing. That human beings would morph into a vegetable state of stupor was one of Cioran's prophecies. Humankind's fetish with technology (knowledge) is an instinctively natural action that takes the form of a narrative(s), i.e., scientific and anthropological, understood as the architectonics of knowledge. From the earliest narratives/myths to the most recent, humans have speculated, invented, and depended on these pseudo-epistemic structures to confront their speculations about their physical and metaphysical environment. It is not my intention to put forth an argument, to debate and play philosophical puzzles; rather, a healthy and earnest dose of skepticism is hoped to jostle the reader, as Kant was jostled by Hume. In this effort, *ennui* and *quotidian* applied to architectonics of knowledge (*narrative epistemic*) paint what is an abashed picture of humanity, one that is humbling and humiliating. Throughout the history of ideas, narratives have been the engine that fuels the continued creation of human knowledge. But, beyond the obvious aforementioned statement, what is humankind's vested interest in narrative discourse? And what role if any does *ennui* and *quotidian* have in human communication?

The world is so exquisite, with so much love and moral depth, that there is no reason to deceive ourselves with pretty stories for which there's little good evidence. Far better, it seems to me, in our vulnerability, is to look Death in the eye and to be grateful every day for the brief but magnificent opportunity that life provides.

—Carl Sagan

What can be speculated about humankind's intellectual evolution and contribution to technological progress is best examined by beginning with the historicity and architectonics of narratives. Narratives are culturally based stories of truth in which knowledge claims are made to seem natural, ultimately seducing humankind with a myopic but seemingly comprehensive vision of their moral purpose/agency, their history and culture. This type of intuitive metaphysical historical and cultural foundationalism is branded in humankind's mind: all things endure and transcend for a discernible *raison d'être*; within this context, narratives, in some cases, function as theoretical fictive stories that are credible and pragmatic enterprises of legitimacy for one's culture.

Hall (1976) is clear about humankind's affinity for model making: "Man is the model-making organism par excellence. . . . The purpose of the model is to enable the user to do a better job in handling the enormous complexity of life" (p. 13). Replete throughout the history of ideas are examples of sages, soothsayers, theologians, philosophers, poets, mathematicians, biologists, economists, physicists, and others who have concocted scientific and anthropological models of explanation to predict and explain that which is critical to the culture's current state of affairs (e.g., Chaos theory, String theory, Marxism). And while these models may dissolve or evolve, the models signify a worldview, a modality of realism and being, for the existence of the given culture. Roszak (1975), commenting on culture, suggested that "it reverberates from mind to mind, and as it does so, it evolves—out and away from its sacred beginning toward new possibilities" (p. 157).

Herder (1966) explained the significance of cultural models through the analogy of a spider web. Spider webs serve as humankind's model/worldview in that language unfolds from within and forms/transforms the dynamic biological and socio-political sphere called culture; this process makes intelligible the inexplicable and metaphysical complexities that humankind confronts. For Herder (1966), language is *thatigkeit*—active, dynamic, and able to create new life forms. It is the foundation from which concepts are born, burgeoned, and acted upon. From this standpoint, narratives, like volcanoes, are violent creative acts that form, transform, and destroy landscapes. Analogously, narratives are ideological mandates and non-negotiable contracts, pressurizing and molding one's being with catechisms that prohibit the wandering of the mind in which all metaphysical and physical problems are solved internally rather than externally. Kluback and Finkenthal (1997) write, "[Narratives become a substitute for reality].We invent a model, a *weltanschauung*, and begin acting upon the world according to its rules" (p. 27).

Historicity of Narratives

The history and dynamism of human thought is really a singular *teleological* narrative in origin germinating from culture. Historically, Western discourse has compartmentalized narratives into two dichotomous intellectual camps, anthropological and scientific (what eventually in modern day is understood as the crisis of knowledge).

The crisis of knowledge, Cassirer (1944) argued, is science (cosmology) pitted against anthropology (biological origin). However, ancient oral cultures (e.g., Sumerians, Babylonians, Egyptians) did not comprehend narrative distinctions based on epistemic approaches or ontological realities. Mathematical and anthropological reasoning were epistemic parts of a whole in the discovery process of the self and humankind's environment. Cassirer (1944) added, "Sense perception, memory, experience, imagination, and *reason* are all linked together by a common bond; they are merely different stages and different expressions of one and the same activity—[humankind's desire to know]" (p. 17).

Western epistemology has gone to considerable lengths to create epistemic bifurcations. Briefly, I will discuss some attributes that mark epistemological and ontological differences between anthropological and scientific narratives. Not only do I believe that humankind's precocious and inquisitive mind is the common denominator of both typologies, but also both typologies signify humankind's endless task of creating *evolved* models and patterns of reliability to understand their role and place within the socio-biological environment and to make conjectures about the physical and metaphysical.

Anthropological Narratives

Anthropological narratives are grounded in the *episteme* of *speculative* thought and exercised by word magic—a significant aspect of human's metaphysical existence, transmitted by means of metaphor and allegory, that shares a consubstantiated relationship with its seeker. Cassirer (1946) explained that word magic occurs when the word, in fact, becomes a sort of primary force, in which all being and doing originate. Frankfort, Frankfort, Wilson, and Jacobsen (1946) reported Speculation—as the etymology [originating from speculative thought] of the word shows is an intuitive, an almost visionary, mode of apprehension. This does not mean, of course, that it is mere irresponsible meandering of the mind.... Speculative thought transcends experience, but only because it attempts to explain, to unify, to order experience. (p. 11)

In other words, anthropological narratives are not dependent on or understood by mathematical/positivist enquiry. Moreover, the relationship between the perceiver and the perceived is anchored in faith, belief, intuition, or some other *supra-episteme*. Frankfort et al. (1946) argued that anthropological narratives are distinct in that they regard man as part of the cosmic ecology, understood as an "I—thou" relationship, rather than a scientific "I—it" relationship.

Scientific Narratives

Scientific narratives denote an important evolution in human thought, signifying an increasing psychological separation of humankind and nature. For the ancients, there was no bifurcation between scientific and anthropological narratives; knowledge was part of the cosmic order of knowledge. However, the Babylonian grasp of astronomy and mathematics proved to be a starting point for what seems to be a subtle epistemic shift in how later civilizations viewed episteme. Instead of humankind sharing an *I–thou* relationship, humankind shares an *I–it* relationship. Characteristic of this relationship is the methodological procedures one utilizes in taking up the question What is a thing, its nature, its, *esse qua esse*—and how does humankind now relates *to* nature, not *with* nature *(I–it)*? An *I-it* relationship, can always be scientifically related to, classified, organized, tested, and isolated within deterministic laws and laws of reasoning. Scientific research is systematic and is guided by positivistic and theoretical modeling about presumed relations among phenomena.

Both anthropological and scientific modes of episteme reveal a great deal about the maturation of human thought. Questions such as who am I, why am I here, and what is this phenomenon clearly have perplexed and continue to perplex humankind. Even more, these questions have not yet been fully realized but are under rigorous investigation via modern anthropological and scientific narratives. Even more, individuals' modes of inquiry have not altogether altered. "In place of myth, we have *history*. In place of magic, *technology*. In place of mystery, *reason*" (Roszak,1975, p. 159).

It is not my intent to provide a pedantic chronological blueprint of all oral cultures and the respective narratives they embrace, but by examining select cultural myththemes and how the narrative is communicated, a modest amount of information is revealed. Common to the worldview of oral cultures—Cassirer (1944, 1946) and others purported—is the creative and transcendental prowess of the spoken word. Gill (1994) noted several Creation myths: Judeo-Christian, Egyptian theologian, Uitoto, Indian, Polynesian, Incan, Quiche Indian, and others' respect for the magic and power of the spoken word. The spoken word brought things into and out of being and allowed access to metaphysical realms. In the section to follow, the Sumerian/Babylonian cultures are explored as the prime example of narrative, myth, and word magic.

Sumerian/Babylonian Narrative Account

Neugebauer (1951) argued that the earliest civilizations were the Sumerian/Babylonian dating back to 5000 BCE evidenced by their historical documented usages of writing. Some expressions of writing existed in the form of tales, law, and mathematical compositions. Neugebauer noted that the Babylonians inherited law and literature from the Sumerians; and in the earliest Sumerian civilization, language appears in the written form predating cuneiform. Although the Egyptians benefited from the Sumerian and Babylonian development of mathematics, Neugebauer noted that the Babylonians were far more advanced than the Egyptians. Babylonians are credited for the first mathematical sexagesimal system. No exact reason why they chose a sexagesimal system (Ifrah, 2000), but the reason probably is related to metrology or astronomy/astrology, according to Cassirer (1944). For the aforementioned reason, both the Babylonian and Sumerian cultures have been looked upon as belonging in the cradle of civilization. The oldest anthropological/cosmological narrative of creationism is the Sumerian narrative of creationism that emerged in 2000 BCE (Roberts, 1993). Gilgamesh is not just a fictitious cataclysmic tale of a flood obliterating a region (this story exists in Old Testament Judaism). The epic of Gilgamesh highlights many prodigious aspects of Sumerian/Babylonian life accounted for in anthropological and historical texts, starting with the power of orality and literacy. Sumerians/Babylonians were among the first to assign gods to various powers of nature (e.g., wind, fire, rain). What is significant about the Sumerian and Babylonian mythology is the emphasis on the spoken word. Marduk, the central God in the Sumerian epic Gilgamesh, spoke the world into existence—"Let my word determine the fates. . . . Let my command be everlasting, and let my word endure!" (Gill, 1994, p.97). In accord with Gill, Heidegger (1992) mentioned, "It is predominately in speaking that man's being-in-the-world takes place" (p. 8E). Roberts (1993) noted

> [Sumerians and Babylonians] later came to ask that religion should help them to deal with the inevitable horror of death. . . . The Sumerians and those who inherited their religious ideas seem to have seen the next world . . . in the notion of Sheol, of Hell (p.44). [I would be remiss in not mentioning, the Book of The Dead, considered to be the earliest and most comprehensive treatise concerning the afterlife by the Egyptians].

Myths offered a temporal/fixed didactic structure that the cultures needed to place in context what seemed to be inexplicable; they also provided a substantial anchor for people's understanding of being in relation to the celestial. As early as 100 BCE, the Sumerians and Babylonians predicted celestial eclipses and eventually the orbits of the sun, distant stars, and planets. Astronomy factored greatly into not only people's understanding of physical cosmology but also their relationship to the gods. The intellect was a whole. Scientific and anthropological epistemes are significant in the Babylonian and Sumerian civilizations in that they assisted individuals' understanding of the gods, the cosmos, the physical environment, and their role in the narrative.

Man must very soon have become aware of the fact that his whole life was dependent on certain cosmic conditions. The rising and setting of the sun, the moon, the stars, the cycle of the seasons—all these natural phenomena are well-known facts that play an important role in primitive mythology. (Cassirer, 1944, p. 68)

Contemporary Narrative Ideology

The term *narrative* in its most basic function is an episteme concerned with rationality, and how meaning is created, sustained, and shared within a social group. Narratives ideally must possess the following qualities: structural coherence, material coherence, characterlogical coherence, and fidelity (Fisher, 1987). Given the communicative truth of this premise, I maintain that even in the 21st century humankind holds fiercely to anthropological and scientific narratives and their *rational* but *mythic* powers. We may not think of them as narratives possessing mythic powers because that would suggest a type of primordial intelligence, and of course, contemporary humans are far too sophisticated. Aren't we?

"Depend upon it, there is [narrative and myth] now . . . only we do not perceive it because we ourselves live in the very shadow of it, and because we all shrink from the meridian light of truth" (Cassirer, 1946, p. 5). Cassier's point is that mythology/narrative never vanishes—it is just subdued. Pass it over as sophomoric, but the power of narrative myth is in the symbolic prowess of consubstantiation—a beacon of clarity, an immediate affirmation of the real or Truth. Knowledge amounts to probable supposition and can never reproduce the true nature of things as they are but must frame their essence in concepts. We never know what a thing is; however, we are aware of our interpretation of what a thing can possibly be. A thing can be classified by its utility, definition, and qualities—its complex and simplest parts; however, these modes of classification belong to the observer's cognitive and linguistic repertoire, not the thing itself. Any expression of a *thing* by humankind—image or linguistic—bares representation of what a thing is to its user, not to the thing in itself. Cassirer (1946) reported von Humboldt's disposition concerning humankind's intimate relationship with language:

Man lives with his objects chiefly—chiefly in fact, since his feelings depend on his perceptions, one may say exclusively—as language presents them to him. By the same process whereby he spins language out of his own being, he ensnares himself in it; and each language draws a magic circle for which there is no escape save by stepping out of it into another. (p. 9)

Whether myth reproduces the nature of the real or Truth, how could one know? Where does one begin such an investigation? Far more important is myth's hypnotic seduction, that inescapable magic circle of gravitation that reels in humankind. With seduction comes duplicity. Symbols allow humans to errantly imagine, lose footing and stumble, and haphazardly acquire knowledge—a blind will to know. Plato's *Protagoras,* Camus (1955) *The Myth of Sisyphus,* Unamuno's (1954) *Tragic Sense of Life*, Nietzsche's (2001) *The Gay Science,* and others have been particularly vociferous on humankind's reckless desire to know even at the cost of self-deception. Duplicity upon duplicity, progress upon progress, utopia upon utopia, there is seemingly no end to the pursuit of Truth. Truth is the dangling ungraspable carrot that taunts us. Boorstin (1961) noted, "We have believed ourselves a nation guided by ideals. Ideals given by tradition, by reason, or by God" (p. 182). There is no logical reason to believe in Truth or truths, but we have to believe in something. Our conceptual being is predicated upon the ruse! Consider, for example, humankind's almost transcendental faith in political, religious, theoretical "isms" and so forth—terms that embody a transcendental narrative and modality of being. Humankind has always been seduced by ideals, new gods, new inanities, new logics, and when their logic no longer suffices our imagination, we sacrifice them according to the gospel of our choice. Burke (1966) declared, "Man is the symbol-using, (symbol-making, and symbol-misusing) animal inventor of the negative (or moralized by the negative) separated from his natural condition by instruments of his own making, goaded by the spirit of hierarchy (or moved by the sense order) and rotten with perfection". (p. 16)

Humankind has packaged and made available upon request just about every story—past, present, and future; and if the future is not present yet, it can be made upon demand! Boorstin (1961) was optimistic when he framed this statement as a question instead of a declaration: "Have we been doomed to make our dreams into illusions" (p. 239)? And is the printing press complicit in the reckless manufacturing and dissemination of seductive narratives and visions of grandeur? In fact, contemporary narrative and myth are almost entirely based on wittingly believing in the fabrication of our own mythos, the invisible foundational pillar in which cultural beliefs are believed to be a part of the natural order of things and thus go unchecked by its adherents (Zizek, 2003); in other words, it is comprehended as organic and not synthetic.

Gill (1994) argued that the transference from mythos to logos meant that art is *not* an imitation of life and that knowledge is purely conceptual—it (knowledge) did not come from the gods. Fundamentally, Gill is correct, but has humankind in earnest ever departed from the umbilical cord? The evolution from mythos to logos is nothing short of a change in the currency—logos is still mythos in terms of humankind's sadistic-addictive and blind-faith relationship to logos, satisfying fundamental human desires, primarily egoism, preservation of the species, and the *will to know* (Boorstin, 1961). Humankind will recreate the story and change history to fit the circle into the square. Truth or self-fulfilling prophecy? Muller (1873) noted,

[The]mythical world is essentially a world of illusion—but an illusion that finds its explanation whenever the original, necessary self-deception of the mind, from which the error arises, is discovered. This self-deception is rooted in language, which is forever making game of the human mind, ever ensnaring it in that iridescent play of meanings that is its own heritage. (pp. 353–355)

The illusion that Muller mentions is the ego or the transcendence of the ego whereby humankind abused God's gift of language to him. By naming, humankind establishes absurdities and convinces ourselves we are not fictions of the mind; we give existence and moral order to things that do not have existence or value to subdue our alienation and anxieties. In my mind, nothing is more needed than for a child to have knowledge that security is present at most times; perhaps the same can be said about humanity's need for consolation and wisdom. But, aren't the two polar opposites? Gleaned from previous sections are three salient points of significance:

(1) Both ancient narrative and myth and contemporary narrative and myth remain grounded in speculative thought (e.g., Burke, Cassirer). Although humankind's tools have morphed in sophistication, always existent between the observer and observant is an ontological barrier called language—this was a primary concern when classifying what a thing is (Cassirer, 1944, 1946; Hope, 1952).
(2) Word magic does not altogether vaporize in the modern era. Words such as *God, socialism, holy war,* and *jihad,* speak to a mode of thinking, being, and action—an invocation of metaphysical ideas followed by human action.
(3) Human thought, primordial and advanced, appears to be hinged on a reckless *desire* or *will* to know.
Q. = Given the previous analysis concerning narrative/myth as an episteme, can narrative contribute to open dialogue; and given different visions of communication, what can be acknowledged about the future of communication?

Ennui and the Quotidian

Ennui provokes a singular topical point that percolated from the 16th century throughout the 18th century critical in narrative studies—the cyclic *quotidian* of existence and the *slowness of time* experienced as self-consciousness. Heidegger (1992) used the term *everydayness* (*die Alltaglichkeit*) to describe what I take to be quotidian and slowness). Make no mistake about it, as a modality of being, *ennui* is always present as a fundamental attunement (*Grundstimmun*) of being; as a field of topic, ennui has recessed into the lexicon of an outdated encyclopedia, from time-to-time referenced as rhetorical prose.

Ennui

Although the linguistic origin of *ennui* has been disputed, scholars concede that the etymology of the word is Latin—*odium* or *odio*—and most probably from the expression "*esse in odio*" (Kuhn, 1976, p. 5). Having continued to evolve from the Middle Ages, *ennui* had two different meanings—that which was sublime and that which was vexing. "In the twelfth to thirteen centuries the word Eneas '*ennui*' signified profound sorrow . . . ; [and in the seventeenth century] *ennui* comes to signify deep spiritual distress" (Kuhn, 1976, pp. 5–6). Examples of *ennui* that provide a clearer context for how I use the word is best understood through the works of Seaver's (1976) assemblage of Beckett's short stories and plays, particularly *Dante and the Lobster*. After providing examples of *ennui*, I apply qualities such as the *quotidian* of existence and the *slowness of being* as they relate to the creation of narratives and their interconnectedness to *das Sein*. Other attributes of *ennui* are slowness, morose joylessness, entropy, unbearable lightness of being, vertigo, and malaise. The following are salient characteristics of *ennui*: "(1) affects the body and the soul; (2) endogenous; (3) [doleful stupor]; (4) estrangement" (Kuhn, 1976, pp. 12–13).

For Heidegger (1992), "Time is [a *human* problem and is conceptualized as] an unfurling whose stages stand in relation of [the] earlier and later to one another" (p. 5E), and so, humans plan and commit to objectives in the unfurling of time that marks how much time has passed, with respect to *dasein* being aware of its own temporality (i.e., death). Emphasized above is an important consequence of time. 'Time as a human construct' is useful in *Zeitvertreib*, driving away the seamless pattern of *ennui* with which time becomes visible in the form of seconds, minutes, hours, days, weeks, months, years, events, and so forth. For without *Zeitvertreib*, humankind, like a fine wine in a decanter, is left to suffer *ennui*, the torpid evaporation of one's being. Heidegger described the sensation of feeling the density of our being slowly increasing:

> We are sitting, for example, in the tasteless station of some lonely minor railway. It is four hours until the next train arrives. . . . We look at the clock—only a quarter of an hour has gone by. . . . Fed up with walking back and forth, we sit down on a stone . . . and in doing so catch ourselves looking at our watch yet again—half an hour—and so on. (Heidegger, 1995, p. 93)

Moreover, because time is a human conceptual construct, it is primarily *pseudo* and illusionary, not affecting the chemical, biological, or physical order of things, although humans characterize it as such. Time amounts to anthropological and scientific fictive narratives about the past, present, and future speculative concerning the on-goings with the human species. Consider the Greeks and the Roman Stoics, especially Aurelius, who advocated on behalf of the importance of examining one's life and obedience to one's civic duty; grounded in this episteme is that the earnest pursuit of self-knowledge by means of philosophical reflection yields wisdom, and a meaningful life is anchored in the *telos* of Western narrative episteme. Influencing such thinking are the questions of how should one conduct oneself in day-to-day living, what is a meaningful life, does the time and space impinge upon humankind's ability to act—all of which germinates from *dasein*. Mentioned earlier, *dasein* is always aware of its finitude, and so it hurries but never escapes ennui, the mirror, in which one sees the diminution of one's being. Heidegger (1992) mentioned, "The end of my Dasein, my death is, not some point at which a sequence of events suddenly breaks off, but a possibility which Dasein knows of in this or that way" (p. 11E). Heidegger's comment speaks directly to the prowess of *dasein's* awareness of its finitude, its temporal existence, and, *ennui*, the eerie shadow and intermittent reminder of the inanity of our pie-in-the-sky narratives. According to Cioran, "*Ennui* shows us eternity which is not the transcendence of time, but its wreck; its infinity . . . a banal absolute where nothing any longer keeps things from turning in circles, in search of their own Fall" (1949, p. 14). It is not by default that Cioran and others attribute the problem of *ennui* with the construction of narratives. Narratives provide a hope, an optimism, a consolation, and an exit from the jaws of death. Without these fabricated narratives, the escape gravity (Truth) of one's existence would instantly vaporize one. "All truths are against us. But we go on living, because we accept them in themselves, because we refuse to draw the consequences" (Cioran, 1949, p. 43). Wittingly, we seduce ourselves into believing that there is a metaphysical foundation beneath our fantasies, a voice of reason to reassure, to guarantee that this debacle will resolve itself; however, nothing awaits us but the coldness of our own inwardness—an inept phenomenology that exists only for those who have invented its hollow layers. Humankind incessantly creates stories upon stories about itself, all hollow, all fallacious, all desperate cries for help. Starry-eyed, humankind looks into the abyss, taking notice that The layers of existence lack density; the man who explores them, archaeologist of the heart, of being, finds himself, at the end of his researches, confronting *empty depth*. . . . Once the veils had fallen, what could they discover but insignificant consequences? *The only initiation is to nothingness—and to the mockery of being alive.* [The narrative], with all of its panoply, is based on our propensity to the unreal, to the useless. . . . Therefore, in order to endure, it seeks to create ever new needs for us, to multiply them without end, for the generalized practice of ataraxia. (Cioran, 1973, p. 12,63)

I have provided a brief introduction to *ennui*, its etymology, its time–space relationship to humankind, what it reveals about knowledge, and why we believe in knowledge.

1. *Ennui* is inextricably bound to *dasein*. *Langeweile* (boredom), or long time, is a metaphysical part of time and shares a relationship with our being (see Heidegger, 1995, 2000); similar to the absurd, *ennui* can only be enumerated.
2. Conventional Western and Eastern narratives emphasize the importance of self-knowledge, or at lease self-awareness. *Ennui* argues the futility in doing so; it also suggests our unflinching desire to be seduced, our addictive will to believe in narrative truths and make narrative truths out of fiction.

The Quotidian of Existence

At first glance, there seems to be a latitude of difference regarding the terms *ennui* and *quotidian*. *Ennui* is the Heideggerian frightening dream before the Cioranian nightmare. *Quotidian* signifies an unimpeded knee-jerk reaction with, not against, life, a go-with-the-flow sensibility understood throughout the observation of Beckett and Kundera, thoughts about the numbness in the on-goings in life (i.e., constant repetition and blandness in which cities look like cities, sidewalks look like sidewalks, and solitude becomes a reminder of our crowded isolation in which nothing happens), which is to say that something has happened because nothing is more real than nothing, space, time, and the filled emptiness that becomes existence. Beckett's *Dante and the Lobster* (Seaver, 1976) underscores the static yet fluid situations that are understood as life, a series of banal observations and an inane mechanistic action of ordered nexts: "First lunch, then lobster, then Italian lesson. . . . What did matter was: one lunch; two, lobster; three, the Italian lesson. That was more than enough to be going on with" (p. 8).

The quotidian, or *die Alltaglichkeit* (everydayness), as identified by Heidegger (1992), is that which is incessantly encountered as movements toward an end—"dealing with the world; tarrying alongside it in the manner of performing, effecting and completing"(p. 7E) in which there lies "no reflection of the ego or the self" (p. 9E). Belacqua (Seaver, 1976) epitomized such behavior in which ritual takes precedence and the discursiveness of time unimpeded unfurls in an ordered set of regular patterns. Take, for example, part of Belacqua's pre-dining ritual—(1) lock the door; (2) deploy a table cloth; (3) light the gas-ring and unhook the flat toaster; (4) cook the toast with an exact science, and so forth. Line by line, Beckett (Seaver, 1976) freeze-frames the invisible minutiae of Belacqua's need for everydayness, underscoring the importance of cadence and his detest for events, people, or actions that obstruct the predetermined order of things. Take the following passage for example:

Now the great thing was to avoid being accosted. To be stopped at this stage and have conversational nuisance committed all over him would be a disaster. . . . If he were accosted now he might just as well fling his lunch into the gutter and walk straight back home. (p. 11)

Belacqua and the average person may find routine comforting, but why? Cultural adaptation provides an orientation of the familiar while reducing the estranged. Cioran offered us three different possibilities: (1) "Man lost the hope of immortality and the drama of salvation of the god-man. It leaves him with rituals he repeats mechanically but no longer believes" (Kluback & Finkenthal, 1997, p. 114), (2) Few things "disturb us more profoundly than the realization that we are held captive by time, that we taste its reality in all that we do and see. No wisdom can free us from the strangling hold it has upon us" (Kluback & Finkenthal, 1997, p. 43); and (3) Man is trapped—"We live trapped between cursed needs to express ourselves and the meaninglessness of our words. Those who do not secrete useless words, but act in silence, are trapped too" (Cioran, 1949, p.180). Cioran's interpretation of humankind's quagmire with time leaves no wiggle room for escape. Humankind is left to asphyxiate on our own unfurling realizations of consciousness; with each unfurling of consciousness, the oxygen we breathe thins until it's depleted.

Ennui and the *quotidian*'s fundamental attunement *(Grundstimmung)* are grounded in *dasein* (Heidegger, 1995). *Dasein* moves from general principles of Being to the most specific category of human existence and includes things that are material and non-material. "Being is not just actual; it is also necessary. Without such an opening up of Being, we could not be human in the first place" (Heidegger, 2000, p. 88). Functionally, how humans relate to themselves, Others, and their environment is conceptually anchored in Heidegger's (2000) primary question from which all philosophical speculation must start—"Why is there being at all instead of nothing?" (p. 2; see Powell, 2006). Thus, the importance of this question is that Being "is the emptiest and thus embraces everything" (Heidegger, 2000, p. 80). Being becomes an inescapable part of the human condition because it embraces all that is, all that is not, and all that is becoming. Both *quotidian* and *ennui* share an interconnectedness with *dasein* in that they are experienced as a part of the fundamental structure of Being and experienced within day-to-day on-goings and contemplation as a consequence, as *das In der Welt sein* (being in the world), which is a critical relation. In my mind, both *quotidian* and *ennui* are terms that blend into one another evidenced by virtue of *das In der Welt sein,* so I will not make any definitive claim as to what precedes the other.

Logically, it should follow that *quotidian* begets *ennui*. Heidegger claimed that we are thrown into the world, are abandoned, and become absorbed into culture—sharing a herd like mentality, exemplar of culture and everydayness. Then, one day *das Was* (the What) happens, the extrication of one from everydayness, and one sees existence for what it is—a complete emptiness. Humankind will find itself naked, paralyzed, staring into space (history) in which nothing happened or happens; and will find that we exist for no other purpose than to exist. This is all too frightening, so we begin where we started—with illusion, narrative, and duplicity.

I will go to some modest detail concerning illusion, seduction, and the narrative relationship. If what I have discussed on the topic of *ennui* is acceptable, then the next logical question is what's next? What happens after humankind sees the futility of its narratives, feels the gravity of its being, and comes to the realization that there is no light at the end of the tunnel? Immediately envisaged from a distance, then in close proximity, is the rut—mind–body dualism, ritual, and plausibly the problems with being born (see Powell, 2006). Literary perspectives from Kundera's (1995) *Slowness* bring clarity to this idea.

In *Slowness,* Vera and her husband are keenly aware of the deluge of Parisians driving through traffic with the urgency of two magnets drawn to one another. Invisible to the hypnotic Parisian drivers, evidenced by the countless accidents the couple avoids, Vera mentions to her husband while referencing a motorcyclist: "These are the same people who manage to be so terrifically cautious when an old lady is getting robbed in front of them on the street" (Kundera, 1995, p. 1). Responding, her husband thinks:

What could I say? Maybe this: the man hunched over his motorcycle can focus only on the present instant of his flight; he is caught in a fragment of time cut off from both the past and the future; he is wrenched from the continuity of time; he is outside time. (Kundera, 1995, pp. 2–3)

On another account, Vera and her husband are having supper. Vera notices a family—a mother, a father, and two children, one of whom is singing loudly—in a restaurant. Their waiter appears to be polite, not irascible or disturbed by the child's behavior. The mother stares at the waiter, as if disgusted because the waiter is ignoring her child. The child then stands up on a chair singing louder, and the waiter unimpeded by the child's tantrum continues his task (Kundera, 1995).

The case for the motorcyclist and the waiter is an unmitigated existence in which space and time collapse and melt into one. Time is thus experienced as duration, a seamless whole, possessing no beginning or no end because it has no length. Activities and plans are reduced to motions and movements within space; things reach a breaking point in which they are absorbed into duration. "All idle talk, that in which such idle talk maintains itself, all restlessness, all busyness, all noise and all racing around breaks down" (Heidegger, 1992,

p. 14E;see also Castaneda, 1971; and Fellini, 1980). There seems to be little recourse for revolt or any meta-activity that critiques, jostles, or gives reason for the gentlemen to pause. Kundera (1995) has implied something important here, maybe prophetic—that humankind is wittingly or unwittingly capitulating the very essence of its uniqueness, refusing to revolt, to draw lines between its biological and conceptual essence—the proverbial distinction humankind has always held in elevated esteem. Refusing to revolt and capitulate, humankind becomes part of the process, the ecological whole (e.g., pond-stream-river-lake-ocean). Could it be that humankind is being wrenched into continuity in which *being* is enveloped by *everydayness* and duration?

"Everything which deals with [duration] inevitably turns into commonplace" (Cioran, 1949, p. 55). Although it's true that with each new narrative comes a new optimism, an inane logic of transcendence, Cioran (1971) noted, "One is and remains a slave [to history] as long as one is not cured of hoping" (p. 102). Why? Charles Newman wrote in Cioran's (1964) *The Fall into Time,* "Man is the only animal who can endure any metamorphosis by putatively explaining it, justify any loss without understanding its implications" (p. 10). Boorstin (1961) suggested that metamorphosis is a result of our extravagant expectations and relentless optimism. "We want and we believe these illusions.... We expect too much of the world. Our expectations are extravagant in the precise dictionary sense of the word—going beyond the limits of reason or moderation" (Boorstin, 1961, p. 3). Moreover, the narrative has to be more seductive—humankind has to create more images and worship them accordingly. Harrington's (1965) text *The Accidental Revolution* argues unequivocally that for more than 50 years things have fallen apart and that idealism has never delivered what it promised. To that end, humankind's fickle relationship to knowledge has been that of a dog chasing its tail. And when idealism fails, as it has throughout history, humankind will invest in another ideal. Harrington (1965) reported literary perspectives regarding this enigma Yeats exclaimed, "The center will not hold"; Roepke spoke of a limitless relativism; Camus asked if society could live without either justice or grace; and Berdyaev added, "The old faith in reason is impotent in the face of irrational forces of history" (pp. 13–15).

Harrington echoed and beckoned Cioran from the grave as many of the thinkers here in this meditation do. If Cioran were alive today, would he cut off his tongue, forever to remain silent, as he abandoned his hand and stopped writing in his later years? In the heights of despair, Cioran asked where do we go from here? What does all this mean? "Wouldn't it be better if I buried my tears in the sand on the seashore in utter solitude? But I never cried, because my tears have always turned into thoughts. And my thoughts are bitter as tears" (Cioran, 1992, p. 34). One is never beyond tears as long as one stays alive! We are bastardized step-children. Neither God nor Satan wants us. Should we kill ourselves? No, because we always kill ourselves too late! Cioran (1992) astutely observed, "You can not escape an implacable fate, and time will do nothing but unfold the dramatic process of destruction; this is the expression of irrevocable agony" (p. 28).

Many points identified regarding the demonic but complimentary tension between *quotidian and ennui* have unfurled. Of significance here is the maze that protects humankind from conscious of itself, similar to what Sartre notated as *en soi,* in which humankind is aware of its own end and is fatigued by the futility of romanticizing and creating another narrative—I have described this as *ennui.* Our end and fate is no different than our father Prometheus—our liver is not torn asunder and made anew again. Ours' is conscious. We are left to see the torpid decay of our being and the rapid decay of our dystopias. Wrenched into the continuity of time, there is nothing to do but to watch our own demise!

Several points were made about the quotidian in this section.

1. Kundera's narrative illustrates paralysis in which humankind unwittingly or wittingly capitulates to the ecological whole and is wrenched into continuity.
2. Although the *quotidian* may vary in its gravitational pull, in which humankind invents new and improved narratives, the *quotidian* never abdicates. Humankind is always a slave to the *quotidian* because of *dasien, das In der Welt sein,* and our incessant hoping.

Thus far, *ennui* reveals the illusion/dystopia that is self-knowledge and the problems with any knowledge—our initiation to nothingness and futility. The *quotidian* illustrates the internalization of that futility, and irrational acts ensue (e.g., wrenched into continuity, suffers hapless optimism).

Final Thoughts: Stupidity

Myth has it that the Israelites wandered hapless in the wilderness for years waiting, hoping, and praying for direction. Theologians have said that God, after some time, heard their prayers and revealed to them his divine will— whether God commanded the Israelites or the Israelites took action recognizing the inanity of their own, how can know ? In *On not wanting to live* and *On death* Cioran (1992) wrote,

At the edge of life you feel that you are no longer master of the life within you, that subjectivity is an illusion, and that uncontrollable forces are seething inside you, evolving with no relation to personal center, or a definite, individual rhythm. (p. 8)

Naivete is the only road to salvation. But for those who feel and conceive life as a long agony, the question of salvation is a simple one. There is no salvation on their road. (p. 25)

Perhaps this is what we and the Israelites felt and continue to feel. Seduced by our optimism for a savior, we endure and endure in hopes of deliverance from ourselves. As long as we remain alive, so does the quotidian and ennui; we are never cured of our suffering, never cured of consciousness. Communication (narrative) is Prometheus's gift to us to endure! He knew all too well that the gods created humankind for their sordid entertainment—we see this exemplified in the book of Genesis and Job with Satan and God deliberating about the affairs of humankind.

Prometheus, the tragic hero, stole so that we might make a mockery out of the gods, by killing ourselves, and by killing ourselves we kill them (God then faces the quotidian and ennui). Or, we can remain drunken in ecstasy, paralyzed in our belief of isms, fables, and narratives! Haven't people realized that all roads lead to death, that language games, knowledge puzzles, and other projects lead nowhere but to their origin, *fear and death*. I am reminded of the knight's lamentation to Death in Bergman's (1957) *Seventh Seal:*

Knight: I want knowledge, not faith, not supposition, but knowledge. I want God to stretch out His hand toward me, reveal Himself and speak to me.

Death: But He remains silent.

Knight: I call out to Him in the dark but no one seems to be there.

Death: Perhaps no one is there.

Knight: Then life is an outrageous horror. No one can live in the face of death knowing that all is nothingness.

Death: Most people never reflect about either death or the futility of life.

Knight: But one day they will have to stand at that last moment of life and look toward the darkness.

Death: When that day comes . . .

Knight: In our fear, we make an image, and that image we call God.

The question that intrigues me is what will happen to our fears, idols, concepts, and their corresponding narratives? Better yet, what becomes of their users? My guess is that humankind will begin where we have ended: Once upon a time there was the profound and sacred. The end.

PROCESSION OF SUB-MEN

—Cioran (1949)

Committed beyond his means, beyond his instincts, man has ended up in an impasse. He has burned his bridges . . . to catch up with his conclusion; animal without a future, he has foundered in his ideal, he has worsted himself at his own game. Having ceaselessly sought to transcend himself, he is paralyzed; and his only remaining resource is to recapitulate his follies, to expiate them, and to commit a few more. . . .

Yet there are some to whom even this resource remains forbidden: "Unaccustomed to being men," they murmur, "do we still belong to a tribe, a race, a breed? So long as we had the prejudice of life, we espoused an error which kept us on a footing with the others. . . . But we have escaped the race....Our lucidity, crumbling our skeleton, has reduced us to a limp existence—invertebrate rabble stretching out on matter to corrupt it with slobber. Behold us among the slime, behold us at that laughable end where we pay for having misused our faculties and our dreams. . . . Life was not our lot: at the very moment when we were drunk with life, all our joys came from our transports above it; taking revenge, life lugs us toward its lower depths: procession of sub-men toward a sub-life . . ." (p. 180)

QUOSUQUE EADEM?

—Cioran (1949)

Forever be accursed the star under which I was born, may no sky protect it; let it crumble in space like a dust without honor! And let the traitorous moment that cast me among the creatures be forever erased from the lists of Time! My desires can no longer deal with this mixture of life and death in which eternity daily rots. Weary of the future, I have traversed its days, and yet I am tormented by the intemperance of unknown thirsts. Like a frenzied sage, dead to the world and frantic against it, I invalidate my illusions only to irritate them the more. This exasperation in an unforeseeable universe— where nonetheless everything repeats itself—will it never come to an end? How long must I keep telling myself: "I loathe this life I idolize?" The nullity of our deliriums makes us all so many gods subject to an insipid fatality. Why rebel any longer against the symmetry of this world when Chaos itself can only be a *system* of disorders? Our fate being to rot with the continents and the stars, we drag on, like resigned sick men, and to the end of time, the curiosity of a denouement that is foreseen, frightful and vain. (p.180-181).

Chapter Four

LUCID DREAMS

Have you ever stared into Eastern European eyes, so many stories, enough stories, so much distance between them and the rest of the world. What color are the tears that bleach their face? Writing is easy for them, since their pens are without ink. Still cursed with branded scars of failed communism, its undeliverable promises, the world offers them a new type of communism—ennui

THE UNIMPORTANCE OF ANYTHING

When you have understood that nothing is, that things do not even deserve the status of appearances, you no longer need to be saved, you are saved, and miserable forever . . .
Only those moments when the desire to remain by yourself is so powerful that you'd prefer to blow your brains out than exchange a word with someone. (Cioran, 1969, p.58, 65).

PIETY

The savior of the world is born, died, born again, died, and stands in front of you—how is it that no one recognizes him.

66   *Chapter Four*

IDLE

Rotate the picture 90 degrees, another 90 degrees, another 90 degrees, and another 90 degrees. You have just experienced Eastern Europe.

(... ENNUI ...)

As we got older we get honester, that's something. And these objective changes correspond like a language to me and my mutations. If the way I see you now is not the way in which we saw you once, if in you what I see now is new it was by self-discovery I found it. I realize that my twenty years might be less than mature. . . . My life has often been by backward glances few personal emotions, thoughts or wishes, and in my life, its even turns and courses, some generous impulse but nothing finished (Yevtushenk, 1963, p.19).

The 'D' Book: Ennui, Quotidian, and Utopianism　　　　67

$$\ldots\ldots X\ldots = \ldots\ldots?$$

All of us, at some moment, have had a vision of our existence as something unique, untransferable and very precious...Self discovery is above all the realization that we are alone: it is the opening of an impalpable, transparent wall — that of our consciousness-between the world an ourselves (Paz, 1985, p.9).

Chapter Five

The 'E' Book—Broken letters and correspondence to and from 'X'

A Letter to X

Each moment, an idea is nurtured and begins to grow; something in us decays and rots. Affirmation and concession are viruses—a transport to utopianism, a mode of zombianism. Cioran, in *All Gall is Divided*, wrote, "We suffer: the external world begins to exist . . . ; we suffer to excess: it vanishes. Pain instigates the world only to unmask its unreality." Cold and vacuous is this reality—it is only warm and verdant in thought. Truth is, Eden never existed, and if it did, Eden has long eroded beyond all recognition. There are no habitants; even God, his adversary, and our first parents' interloper have departed. Memories of utopianism are the only refuge—praying for another life . . . only to destroy what has been made anew.

Spewed from the mouth of our Father and into nothingness, humankind upholds the tradition and task of idle-making—stories/knowledge of grandeur—in which we have become quite proficient. Having acquired neither the acumen nor the will to hull precious medals to the incinerator, I have succumbed to silently protesting my indifference to humankind's inanity, realizing that every Truism will rendezvous with its truth.

—G.A. Powell
eulogy to be read. . . .

*

Gerald,

It seems as though you're really coming into your own sphere of philo-intellecutal prowess. I'm very pleased. It's a part of you that was always alive and well at University X, but not very much encouraged, unfortunately. It's pleasing to see that you are applying original and controversial insight into your research. I don't recall anyone ever thinking and positing ideas quite the way you do. Sophie was different, a clipped model of what the department wanted. You're counter, the kind of academic rupture so sorely needed in most universities. Certainly, "en soir" et "pour soir" will be headings somewhere in your paper! Sartre. I see he continues, like the rest of the exsitentialists, to interest you. I was going to formulate, in fact, a paper based on Camus' "L'étranger." I still might.

I would love to assist you in the preparation of your work. Definitely. Hmmmm . . . but I wouldn't call myself a photographer:) Critiquing existentialist elements in photos is one thing . . . I rather like the concept. Sounds Barthesian. You do know his book "Camera Lucida," don't you? If not, check it out. He discusses his ideas on photos and the "dictum/stratum," I think it is, in each of them. Interesting. Take a look at it. Also if I've not recommended Gaston Bachelard to you, let me do so now. It is imperative that you find and read his _Poetics of Space_ book. You need that as part of your intellectual repetoire. It's a wonderful book.

Continue to fill me in on the status of your work. I don't want to miss a beat. You're reference should arrive late this week, the postman said.

Siempre,
X

*

Hi, G.,

When you're ready for me to critique what you've written thus far, just send me an attachment. It would be a pleasure reading your critical work :)

X

*

Hi, Gerald,

You can now write me at this e-mail, Gerald. I put your letter in the mail today. I think it may take a week. And I hope you get this post at BC. Why do you want to leave St. Joseph's already? Curious. Also, do you still have MY reference letter on file? Can you e-mail it to Kristen. She "seems" interested in wanting a complete dossier from me. Keep in mind, Gerald, that applying for academic posts anywhere can be an "iffy" business. I'll include XXX address below so, if need be, you can delete any former addresses in your reference of me in order to include hers:

X,X

Department of Southern Illinois University at Carbondale Carbondale IL 62901-6605
Keep me abreast of BC! lots of love,

X

*

G,

I did find the book by Ludivic, I must read it so we can critique it together

*

GP

We must continue this conversation!!!! Your comment pertaining to the bourgeois educated is exciting. If you reference Jacques Ellul's text on Propaganda and Persuasion: the formations of men's attitudes, he will share the same concern. I'm hungry, so I will return to the issue later. One more thing, would you like for me to send you job postings from "Spectra"—the communication magazine. The listings are rather new and there are a couple of openings in NYC. . . Have you considered the New School, or lecturer positions at the University of Chicago? Multiple openings exist.

*

GP

I believe the quote is from —Opinons and Beliefs.
One of the most constant characteristics of beliefs is intolerance. The stronger the belief, the greater the intolerance. Well said. I happen to agree. Beliefs are ideas and ideas can be either revolutionary or unimportant. Men dominated by certitude cannot tolerate those who do not accept it.
—Gustave Le Bon.

*

X

Is that from _Pscyhology of the Masses_? Yes, the truth is you are American but, and I am assuming, you do not feel like an American. Oh, I'm profoundly American as I often say just to annoy my French friends. But I do feel the same way about America at times, you're right.

*

Chapter Five

GP

Like Cioran, and I thank you so much for the read, an intellectual has no nationality. I would go so far as to say the same is true with you. My question for you is would not the trite Aristotelian and intellectual in you and me fall victim to Le Bon's dictum.

*

X

Yes, I think so. But I am not always dominated by "certitude" if by "certitude" one can substitute one's view of the world, then yes I am dominated by "skepticism" which is a certitude for me and without which I could not function. And I think everyone should be skeptical; I'm often shocked by navieté, especially from the bourgeois educated. One of my purposes as an educator is to provoke. And any good intellectual should know that his purpose is to provoke, in my humblest of opinions. amitiés et j'suis pas français!

X

*

GP

As always you have been supportive which is encouraging. Three weeks ago, maybe longer, you mentioned—Paris is great, yet you feel numb. I realize that you have been there for a much longer time than I have been at Saint Joe, but the numbness is the same.

*

X

Yeah, the numbness for me though is a kind of psychological isolation or drain, Gerald which is only felt by living and interacting in a foreign country, something that dear old useless University could not have taught me. Adaptation does not happen overnight. It, too, is a psychological process. I speak French, for example, fluently. But a lot more is required when waking up and going about your business in another country like camouflaging French sensibility which I cannot do. I'm too psychologically American. And, besides, pretending to be French is not my forté. But nothing is always black and white, is it? I love Paris. It is an intellectual's dream to live and work here. You would love it. What can make it hard, however, is the French resistance and stubbornness to just about everything. It's always fashionable to say "no" in France:)

*

GP

No institution will provide me with the stimulation I need. Everyone is or wants to be a teacher and no one desires to be a student.

*

X,

I think that's profound what you just said. No one wants to be a student. Does being a student mean being "demoted" or "secondary" or maybe even "irrelevant?" I love being a student. And I take pride in not being an "expert" in and on all things. The student position should be an enviable one. And I have too many questions in my head that won't stop which forces me into the humble position of "student." It's a gift to be so.

*

GP

Here people are fixated with superficial issues such as who is having the potluck this week. No one wants to settle down and deal with ideas. I value our time together and look forward to reading your e's because they remind me of a time when I was dead and how lucky I am to be alive.

*

X

The question of "who's doing the pot-luck this week" is surely a metaphor for something else, isn't it? I should hope so. But, then again, perhaps this is that usual, stale, professorial repartée amongst faculty that's designed to see if one is a) a team player and b) team material. Stuff like this is harmless bullshit extant , it seems, only among faculty. Yes, yes!! bring your ideas! You and I may have started some kind of new philo-intellecutal exchange here via internet for the first time. So what's on your mind? And how's your paper coming along? I'm still working on an identity idea

Love,
X

*

GP

'On Symbolic Discourse'

Symbols are never negotiated, just augmented. Hmmm. I used to believe in the concept of identity and perhaps I still do. Tell me something—from reading Baudrillard and Derrida, doesn't the idea of symbolic implosion or linguistic implosion occur. I might be wrong X, but metaphysically, language can no longer support synthetic human experiences.

*

X

Of course not!! Language can never fully encapsulate the human experience; it can only suggest it. It can only be used as a symbolic tool, if nothing else. Higher truths, incidentally, do not rely upon language as a mediating device. Higher truths, be they emotional or intellectual, operate within different realms of cognition in which language would be too slow and superfluous.

*

GP

We are left to conceptualizing . . . identity as a fictitious narrative, a historical account of egoism. You are definitely on to something.!!! But you were always brilliant.

*

X

Gosh, Gerald, please! Stop referring to me as brilliant and other such ego-serving references :) Identity. What is identity, as it is often asked? To define it would be to limit it. But we need to limit it, to draw it, to corner it. The only "identity," I argue, that any of us have ever had and can be certain of is our "physical body." It is the only "self" that is constant and of which we can be "certain." The only "tangible identity" there is. Too bad it has to perish . . . The rest of identity is psychology.

*

GP

X, I sent your letter via snail mail, but I didn't get a receipt of confirmation from the US postal. Please check with Brunel ASAP. I'm sure they received the e-letter.

*

X

Thanks, again, Mr. (Dr.?) Powell for snail-mailing the letter to Brunel. I thought it'd be good that they receive an "e-letter" and one by regular mail. I am going to London next week, in fact, just to "show my face" and let them know that I'm serious about posting my candidature for the position, which is just a lecturer's position, btw. I need forward motion at this point in my life and, at times, French culture is too keen on leisure and unkeen on advancement and ambition. That simply isn't the culture, fortunately or unfortunately :) :(

*

GP

I find it terribly difficult to write anything good these days; its almost as if Aristotle's and Socrates' hands are my hands. Just to keep current, I am writing a paper on black identity, film, and so on!!! :o(I am also trying to write an article about Bergman!! The whole research and teaching game does not seem appealing to me. I prefer, as you did or still do, to drink wine, cafe, talk, and rest.

*

X

Yeah, I know what you mean here. I like the idea of sitting in a café, smoking, philosophizing, drinking à la française. But after a while, there's something in me that demands motivation, another neglected or unknown concept within French mentality. They're very rooted in a 19th century, Cartisian sensibility. And more power to them, I guess. But it's good to stop and smell the roses now and again. I think you'd make a great teacher, Gerald. Why does the teaching game not interest you so? Researching one's concepts for publication is always going to be the more interesting of the two, IMHO. You'll be fine. If you can survive University X, you can survive Indiana.

*

X

Hi, Gerald, Well, thanks for the mention at St. Joseph's, Gerald. Yes, Europe is my home for now. Wherever there is an opportunity to expand myself, I'm there. I'll keep you posted.

*

GP

X, no problem!! I thought you would follow Paris to your grave. Why England? X, there is nothing you can do for me, but to offer your friendship. :o) Take care and stop calling me Dr. Powell. When we converse it's human.

Gerald

*

X

Hi, Gerald, instead of "Dr. Powell." Yes, I WILL follow Paris to my grave. But I think I need a break. I'll write you soon. Siempre,

X

*

GP

Either you are entirely modest, romantic, or none of the above. Never had I known you to be modest :o), but romantic, X, is always the case. Yes, 135 pages on Spike Lee seems suspect, but the dissertation was an exploration of ideas about semiotics to a degree. Far too much credit was given to Spike Lee—symbolic linguistic, etc. . . metaphor and so on. Give me a break!!!! Parts of my dissertation play with the Italian semiotician—Umberto Eco, other parts of it mimic Pierce. There is no guise hear. The dissertation, at the least, never was about Lee, black identity, or Gerald, it was an intertextual juxtaposition of thoughts which appear to be together, but never say too much about anything.

*

X

Well, I like the way you explained the above. Surely, I said to myself that your dissertation, it is after all such, was than just a cursory look into Spike Lee films. I just love the way you reference authors and semioticians like Eco. You think your former department's heard of him. Like they probably haven't heard of Bergman?

*

GP

One's first read of Cioran is mind blowing. At times I thought he was Christ holding a dialogue with God the Father. At other times, you could make an argument for him as Satan talking to Christ. The question for me is this. Why does he spend so much energy debasing God, Saints, philosophers etc... This is not a problem for me. Beneath his poetic and sadistic undertones is an actual cry for salvation.

*

X

Cry for salvation? Who? Cioran? Oh, no, no, no. That's not Cioran. He teases; he seduces. He speaks the truth, too. And he's always worth the read.

His book titles are better in French though i.e., _The Trouble with Being Born_ in French is _L'inconvénient d'etre né_ sounds much better to me. In America, we call this displaced anger. Really, I do like him!! As he states in T.O.S. God I can't live with you or without you.

Hope all is well with you in your transition to the mid-West. They should love you out there.

siempre también,
X

*

GP

X, there is nothing to like :o) To be quite frank with you, the prose, the proofs, and structure of the dissertation suck.

*

X

still don't understand why you "had" to write on Spike Lee films. It just seems beneath you. You certainly manage the academic prose of it all. But so far, part of me doesn't "believe" your proofs or the necessity in writing it, your dissertation. It is a dissertation, right? At 135 pages, I'm impressed, if not suspicious.

*

GP

Who turned you on to Cioran, and what do you admire about his writing?

*

X

XXX, do you remember him? turned me on to Cioran. Cioran moved to Paris in 1935 and began writing aphorisms from then on. He's very well known here as are many post-war intellectuals who came to Paris. Cioran's a combo of Buddhist thought and existentialist brooding, so you're right on the Camus comparison. I think Cioran even read Camus' "L'étranger," I'm not sure. Hope all is well. One last question: were you really advised NOT to write about Bergman?? I've told this story to a few colleagues here who were absolutely horrified to hear something like this.

Anyway, take care.
Love,

X

*

X

Hi, Gerald,

I know you're busy with your move to Indiana. But I just, for the first time, read your dedication page of your dissertation and am impressed that you would mention me in the same breath as the other Greats mentioned. I will thoroughly let you know what I liked and did not like about your dissertation. I'm sure I can be frank with you, yes?

Love,

X

*

GP

About the departments take on my dissertation, Bergman was a condition they set for me. I wasn't to explore any Nordic "white" discourse. I fell into a deep state of depression—contemplated suicide. Not good, but I made the best of it. Life after University X has presented many opportunities

*

X

Why does the above not surprise me in the least? It would be just like the department to hinder, prevent and impede the intellectual development and curiosity of its graduate students. What assholes supreme!!! Bergman would've been too much of a challenge for the intellectually-challenged teaching staff in the communications department. How sad. How very fucking sad. Don't they realize that having an African American write a dissertation on Bergman would not only make you look good, but the school as well? Imagine an employer looking at your CV and being somewhat impressed that you wrote on Bergman as opposed to the stereotypical, fucking predictable topic of tired-ass Spike Lee!! I forgot why I couldn't recommend University X. Now I know!! Sorry that you had to waste your time on Spike Lee at the expense of your rather closed-fucking-minded committee, who're nothing but hacks anyway. This is proof of it! No "nordic discourse" please! They succeeded in temporarily stunting your growth. I supposed they felt you should be as ignorant as they on the subject of Bergman, huh? Oh, well . . . By the time you read this, you should've successfully defended your thesis. So congratulations Dr. Powell.

And I will definitely look into the European Graduate School.

*

GP

Hey X,

You are absolutely right about University X U. Like you, there is nothing intellectually challenging that is offered. I have often turned to the courts of coffee shops and occasional travels to learn about culture, philosophy and other ideas. These people you mentioned are new to me. I have never heard of them; I will definitely have to read them soon! I am just too sorry that University X did not appreciate your talents, but I am not surprised at all. In many ways, I would like to continue my formal education, but formal education is stifling. All formal education is repressive; it aims to stifle the human spirit. Even Camus, Sartre and Dostoyevsky (sp) carried disdain for academia. If you read The fall and Notes from the underground, the absurdity of education and existence are recurring motifs.

On a lighter note, you probably won't believe it, but I am getting married on March 6, 2003. Like Fydor states—I live to satisfy my full capacity to live. I told her about you and she is excited about meeting you. She also holds you in high regard. Hopefully, we all can meet, and we can have one more class together. Terence, I am not making an idle out of you, but your influence on me is something of an enigma. I have been exposed to so many interesting ideas and people. My doctoral dissertation is titled—A rhetoric of symbolic identity: An analysis of Spike Lee's X and Bamboozled. It is not anything that I feel proud of, but I have explored some issues in semiotics and formation of identity and negotiation. Although my dissertation is novice, I would be honored if you would look at it—and please be brutal. I will e-mail it to you tomorrow.

*

X

Hi, Gerald,

Firstly, why in the world would you feel indebted to someone like me? Of course, I did and DO enjoy my conversations with you and sometimes wondered why the both of us were ever at University X to start with, with its bold and brave nonsense about education. I warn you, though, I am not perfect:)

You're getting married? So soon? You have my congratulations and best wishes. Marriage has not yet seriously entered the equation for me. I am not against academia, per se. But I do see its limitations and often speak out against these. My academic experiences have not been rosey ones, sad to say.

Your dissertation has to do with Spike Lee instead of Ingmar Bergman??? What???????? Did your committee somehow feel lost when reading about

Bergman? Did they even know who he was or is? Spike Lee? Don't get me wrong, I'm a huge fan; but I'm not sure Spike would make for proper thesis material on the doctoral level. Maybe an article in a peer review mag . . . He seems too recent and without appropriate substantive depth for the undertakings of a doctorate. I could be wrong, though. Do send it to me anyway, when you have the chance. A doctorate on Bergman would have given you *more* of an international flavor. But don't worry, you'll be stellar in your defense. And I will be with you in SPIRIT!

Love,

X

*

GP

You are amazing! You are writing a dissertation in French.

*

X,

Hi, Gerald, and yes I have an interest in writing a French doctorate primarily to assuage the mistake in getting one at University X. I don't want you to get the impression that I think of University X often. I don't. I realize that I wasted much time there in being taught next to nothing. I cannot recommend University X to anyone, unfortunately. It's an entirely different cultural perspective living and working in another country. It's an education unto itself. I recall very few people at University X being able to swallow the fact that I would be teaching at the Sorbonne here, nothing of the sort had ever happened. And, of course, the congratulations were few and far between. You know I still read Burke and Aristotle, but I must confess, my reading habits have shifted more toward European intellectuals, past and current. And everyone, even the garbage men, think they are intellectuals in Paris. Europe's history is much older as you know and the people tend to be more literate than Americans. Anyway today I find myself reading the likes of Kundera, Cioran, Yourcenar, etc. I certainly, by the way, would love to read your thesis and critique it. Hope all is well with you Gerald, and let's try to keep in touch.

Love,

X

*

GP

What's up X? The answer to your first question is no. My dissertation is not in final form. I hope next Monday the document will be completed. As far as life after University X, I look forward to working in Indiana. St Joseph' College offered me a tenor track position. I only teach courses in rhetorical theory and philosophy. The irony is I'm tired of school. I have other hobbies and interest that I would like to pursue. Similar to you, books will always assuage the mind, but coffee and wine are the keys to the soul!

X

*

Hi, Gerald,

It's good to hear that things are winding down for you. I know working and finishing a dissertation is a long haul. I, in fact, am thinking of writing another in French this time. Where is St. Joseph's College exactly? I know you'll feel more at ease once you leave the University X environment; I still recall how repressive and tiring it was. Look forward to expanding your horizons. You'll be successful. By the way, who was the contact person's name at St. Joseph's? Could you pass his name and e-mail address on to me? He may be able to refer me to a possible contact somewhere in the midwest or elsewhere. My plans, of course, are to remain in Europe to pursue "academia" here. I would like to part of the African American studies department in Tours. Anyway, I try to keep my options open.

So when is the defense? And do right me when it's over with all of the details please. Can you believe I'm currently reading a series of interviews of Bergman, in French of course.

Speak to you soon, Dr. Powell.

References

Bergman, I. (Director). (1957). *Seventh seal* [Film]. (Available from Svensk Filmindustri, Stockholm, Sweden.)
Boorstin, D. J. (1961). *The image: A guide to pseudo-events in America.* New York: Vintage Books.
Breton, A. (1969). *Manifestos of surrealism.* Michigan: University of Michigan Press.
Burke, K. (1966). *Language as symbolic action.* Berkeley: University of California Press.
Cage, J. (1961). *Silence: lectures and writings.* Connecticut: Wesleyan University Press.
Camus, A. (1946). *The stranger.* New York: Random House.
———. (1955). *The myth of Sisyphus.* New York: Vintage.
Cassirer, E. (1944). *An essay on man: An introduction to a philosophy of human culture.* New York: Doubleday Anchor.
———. (1946). *Language and myth.* New York: Dover.
Castaneda, C. (1971). *A separate reality.* New York: Washington Square Press.
Cioran, E. (1949). *A short history of decay.* New York: Arcade.
———. (1964). *The fall into time.* Chicago. Quadrangle.
———. (1969). *The new gods.* New York: Quadrange.
———. (1971). *Drawn and Quartered.* New York: Arcade.
———. (1973). *The trouble with being born.* New York: Arcade.
———. (1991). *Anathemas and admiration.* Londaon: Quartet Encounters.
———. (1992). *On the heights of despair.* Chicago: Chicago University Press.
Cusa, N. (1960). *The vision of god.* New York: Frederick Ungar Publishing Co.
Fellini, F. (Director). (1980). *8 1/2* [Film]. (Available from Corinth Films).
Finkenthal, M., & Kluback, W. (1997). *The temptations of Emile Cioran.* New York: Peter Lang.
Fisher, W. R. (1987). *Human communication as narration: Toward a philosophy of reason, value, and action.* Columbia: University of South Carolina Press.

Frankfort, H., Frankfort, H. A., Wilson, J. A., & Jacobsen, T. (1946). *Before philosophy: The intellectual adventure of ancient man.* Hammondsworth, Middlesex, Baltimore: Maryland Penguin.

Gill, A. (1994). *Rhetoric and human understanding.* Prospect Heights, IL: Wavelength Press.

Hall, E. T. (1976). *Beyond culture.* New York: Doubleday.

Harrington, M. (1965). *The accidental century.* New York: Macmillan.

Heidegger. M. (1992). *The concept of time.* Malden, MA: Blackwell.

———. (1995). *The fundamental concepts of metaphysics: World, finitude, solitude.* Bloomington, IN: University of Indiana Press.

———. (2000). *Martin Heidegger: Introduction to metaphysics.* New Haven, CT: Yale.

Herder, J. G. (1966). *On the origin of language: Two essays by Jean Jacques Rosseau and Johann Gottfried Herder.* New York: Fredrick Ungar.

Hope, F. (1952). *Aristotle metaphysics.* New York: Columbia University Press.

Ifrah, G. (2000). *The universal history of numbers: From prehistory to the invention of the computer.* Hoboken, NJ: John Wiley & Sons.

Kuhn, R. (1976). *The demon of noontide: Ennui in western literature.* New Jersey: Princeton University Press.

Kundera, M. (1995). *Slowness.* New York: HarperCollins.

Muller, F. M. (1873). *The philosophy of mythology: Introduction to the science of religion.* London: Kessinger.

Nietzsche, F. W. (2001). *The gay science.* United Kingdom Cambridge University Press.

Neugebauer, O. (1951). *The exact sciences in antiquity.* New York: Dover.

Paz, O. (1961). *The Labyrinth of solitude.* New York: Grove City Press.

Powell, G.A. (2006). Communication, alienation, and the other: An ontological view of interpersonal communication. *Communication Annual, 62,* 50–64.

Roberts, J. M. (1993). *A short history of the world.* New York: Oxford University Press.

Roszak, T. (1975). *The Aquarian frontier and the evolution of consciousness: Unfinished animal.* New York: Harper & Row.

Seaver, R. W. (1976). *A Samuel Beckett reader.* New York: Grove City Press.

Taylor, C.C.W. (1996). *Protagoras.* London: Oxford University Press.

Unamuno, M. (1954). *Tragic sense of life.* New York: Dover.

William, J. (1956) [1897], *The Will to Believe and Other Essays in Popular Philosophy,* Dover Publications, New York.

Yevtushenko, Y. (1963) *Yevtushenko selected poems.* Baltimore: Penguin.

Zizek, S. (2003). *The puppet and the dwarf: The perverse core of Christianity.* Cambridge, Massachusetts: The MIT Press.

www.ingramcontent.com/pod-product-compliance
Lightning Source LLC
Chambersburg PA
CBHW031555300426
44111CB00006BA/324